A MATCHSTICK

A journey through time k

By Alan Simpson

Copyright @ Alan Simpson

2017

Alan Simpson asserts the moral right to be identified as the Author of this Work, in accordance with the Copyright, Design and Patents Act 1988

Published on behalf of Alan Simpson by Alan Rigby

Bolton 2017

ISBN 978-0-9935795-2-3

I

My Thanks to

Kath Addis

Paul Salveson

John & Carol Barnard

Graham Holt

Alan Rigby

Janet Shaw

Margaret Koppens

Bernice Crank

Terry Higginson

James Kidd

David Mason

Malcolm & Nikki

Turton Local History Society

(Bolton Market Place)

Peter Street

Eddie Thompson

Norman Hindley

Derek Worthington

Pat & Dave Smith

Ron Horsley

Frank Gayley

The late :-

Derek Billington

Clive Walsh

Bert Jones

Peter Nightingale

Cyril Bracegirdle

Bob Porter

Appreciation for photographs

Halliwell Local History Society

Bolton News

Clifton Country Park

I dedicate **"A Matchstick's Journey"** to my old friend, the late David Bromley

"Thanks for the memories David"

Alan Simpson - May 2017

Photographs

To

THE FAIRHURST FAMILY.

Best Wishes

Arthur Simpson

[signature]

VII

POEMS - MY THANKS TO POETS

A MATCHSTICKS JOURNEY

My Grandpa Bill Peters loved to walk. He walked eight miles a day, five or six days a week, from his home in Halliwell to his work as a Crofter at Harwood Vale Bleachworks, near Bolton, where he worked for sixty years. After he retired in 1954, my mother worked out that he had walked approximately 130,000 miles during his working life, an incredible achievement.

From being a little lad of four I walked many miles with Grandpa. It was 1946 and I was eight years old when he said **"right lad next Saturday, if it's a nice day and't "Wanderers" are playing away, I'm goin't tek thi tert "Brunt Edge Pit"** (Burnt Edge Mine on Smithills Moor). Saturday arrived it was a pleasant early Autumn day. Mam prepared our 'butties' and a bottle of Dandelion and Burdock and we set off from Grandpa's house in Halliwell just after breakfast. The walk would take us most of the day, the first part of which would take us up Halliwell Road, then the long climb up Smithills Dean Road to where it meets Scout Road. We crossed over to Coalpit Road and walked a further mile to 'Roscoe's Farm', probably the oldest building on the Moor. The datestone on the building reads '1768'. At Roscoe's we turned left, heading down the valley by a fast running stream. To our right a distinctive bracken covered hill came into view, Grandpa said **"That's Sugar Loaf Hill Lad"**. The hill is a 'Cairn' or ancient burial ground, although no evidence has been found to substantiate this. There are other 'Cairns' scattered across the Moors, such as 'Two Lads' 'Pike Stones' 'Noon Hill' and 'Round Barrow' discovered as recently as 1956. It is thought there may be others as yet undiscovered. As we walked on the surrounding landscape was changing, it became noticeably less green and the vegetation became quite sparse. The path followed the stream to a point where we came to what remained of a building. Seeing this Grandpa shouted **"Here we are lad, its Brunt Edge Pit".** It was approaching midday, so it was time to eat our 'Butties' and we sat down on a large boulder by the stream. All I could hear was the sound of water tumbling down the valley to our left. I was disappointed. I expected the sound of miners working and horses pulling heavy carts but it was obvious, even to me as a young lad, that this had not been a working mine for many years. In fact my later research showed that 'Burnt Edge' originally known as 'Newfield Colliery' ceased production in the early 1930's and the entrances to the mine were sealed but some local lads discovered that the mine could still be entered by an adit lying off a nearby path. They gained entry to the mine and they rode on small railway wagons that had been foolishly left behind when the Pit closed, how did they do that in absolute darkness? A highly dangerous 'Game' to play.

Grandpa was a pipe smoker, as most older men were at the time. When he finished eating, he took out his pipe and tobacco pouch, filled the pipe with 'Thick Black Twist' a very strong tobacco, which, when lit produced a pleasant aroma (I can still smell that smoke and I still have his Tobacco Pouch almost seventy years later). He used a couple of matches to get the pipe going. He then lit a third match, extinguished it immediately and said **"If I drop this matchstick into this little river it'll finish up in't Sea"?** whereupon he dropped the match into the stream. As the matchstick quickly disappeared over a small waterfall to the valley below, I asked Grandpa **"Will it ever get ter't Sea Grandpa"?** He replied **"You bet it will Lad"**. Grandpa was never wrong.

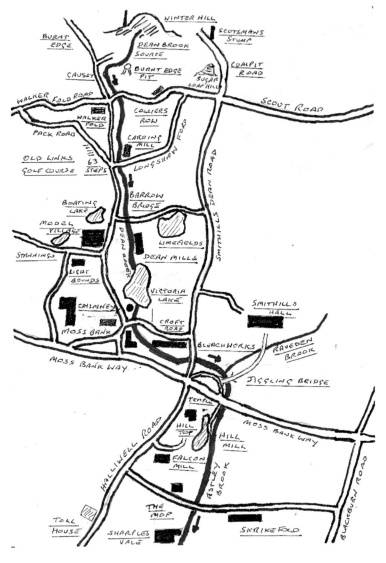

Map 1 Dean Brook

I never forgot that September day at 'Brunt Edge' and so some seventy years later I decided to return to that spot by the stream and follow it from it's source high on Winter Hill, to the sea, as the matchstick would have done in 1946. It would have passed through a varying landscape and many places of historical interest along the way, a distance of nearly fifty miles.

In September, 2015 the same time of year as my previous visit, my starting point was not Coalpit Road but I would approach Burnt Edge from Walker Fold. I followed the path leading west over Smithills Moor (with a box of matches in my pocket) and onto the barren landscape of Winter Hill. Along the 'Causey' or Causeway of quite large gritstone slabs. How many men and horses got them there and laid them is incredible. They were made smooth by numerous walkers and in the 18th and 19th Centuries by the hundreds of Miners and Quarrymen who walked miles along this well used path to the mines and quarries scattered across the Moor. Passing Walker Fold Woods to my right, an area of Pine and Larch trees straddled the valley to the brook below. After a steady climb of approximately half a mile I arrived at a gate, after which the path divides to the right and leads to the old pit where the matchstick's journey began. The path ahead leads along Burnt Edge, over the Moor and onto Winter Hill. At this point I paused for a while admiring the dramatic landscape unfolding before me and was reminded of a poem, written in dialect by Anne Fleetwood over thirty years ago. She writes

GOOIN WUM T'WINTER HILL
Written by Anne Fleetwood in 1982

When aw lived up Winter Hill, mun a bin fifty yar back,
We usd to goo bi Georges loan or else bi't Brunt Edge track.
Fro Georges Loan thro' Ramwell's Farm, pass t' Pit and Quarry
too,
Reawnd a corner - stop for breath; Eeh! What a lovely view.
Then, on past t' Butts and up thro't'cut, th' owd brick kiln comes
in seight.
Deawn't track we goo, thro't garden gate at last we're wum for
neight.
'Hole Bottoms' was the name o't place at t'top o't 'rough yewn
track.
It tuk us half an heawr t' get up only twenty minutes back.

Now t'other road we''d tak somedays, wi weather feign and
warm,
Thro' Barrow Bridge, then up yon steps to Walker Fowt bi t'
farm.
Across the road an 'ower style (we never oppent gate)
Along Brunt Edge and deawn to t' bruck, crossed even when in
spate.
Past Sugar Loaf an' up thro t'glen and then another style,
The little stream to cross agen; we're wum for t' rest awhile.

On other days we'd 'ave a change, instead of gooin' up t' steps
We'ed goo up t' road that crossed t' Golf Links to t' farm that
Morrises kept.

'Hole Hill' 't was named as I recall, , then on alung top road b't wall
Past t' place they cawd "Slack Hall,", deawn t' hill agen to t' babblin bruk
Crossed wi' a bit o' luck, the rest o't way we'en bin befooer back wum agen once mooer.
There's mony a tale I'ave to tell bout yon Smithills Moor
O Grouse and Germans, whinberry pie,aye, pages scooer on scooer.
It would take me quite a spell an awm seventy now, what's mooer
So, I'd better get it down reight quick afore they shut the dooer.

Winter Hill is a relatively modern name. Standing over a 1000 feet above Horwich in the west and Belmont in the east. Maps of the 17th and 18h Centuries show it as 'Egberden Hill',earlier documents from the 13th century refer to it as 'Wintyrhold' and 'Wintyrheld'. The early Kings of Northumbria and Lancashire, hunted these hills, which at that time was heavily forested and it is very likely that thousands of years ago people lived in these forests, hunting wild boar and foraging to survive. This could be Lancashire's earliest civilization going back to the bronze age. Some years ago, in an area known as 'Tigers Clough', a flint axe head was found in a river bed dating to around 2000 B.C. These hills were created by glacial actions many years ago and three tributaries from springs formed the source of, as we know them to-day, Dean Brook, Dakins Brook and the River Douglas.

There are two seams of coal under Winter Hill and over the years these have been extensively mined, leaving some parts of the moor dangerously unstable. During the 18th and 19th centuries there were half a dozen working pits, mainly located on the south side of the hill. Such as Holdens Colliery, Montcliffe, Winter Hill Colliery, Wilderswood and the Mountain Mine, operated by J. Crankshaw & Company, opened in 1860 and closed in 1908. Burnt Edge was one of the last to close. There was also extensive quarrying towards Smithills Moor in the East.

In the distance above Wilders Moor is 'Two Lads' also known as 'Wilder Lads' two memorial cairns. There are different opinions as to why they were erected. Thomas Hampson in 1883 described 'Two Lads' as the graves of two children of a Saxon King and recorded that Winter Hill was once called 'Edgar Hill. More recently, it has been said that the Cairns mark the site on which some 400 years ago, two young boys lost their way in a snowstorm and died of exposure.

Figure 1 The site of Holdens Colliery

A gate to my left opens onto a path leading to Moor Road which joins Georges Lane. There were three separate dwellings on the moor given the name 'Hall' even though one was no more than a cottage. 'Slack Hall' had been a farmhouse and 'Sod Hall', both located on this road above Burnt Edge was a small farm, so named because it was in such a dilapidated state, the wind blew through the gaps in the stonework and the owners resorted to filling the gaps with 'sods' of earth to keep the warmth in. The third, 'Ouzel Hall' was quite a large building, more to the west, which I will describe later.

Heading towards the highest point on the moor is the site of the old Brick and Tile Works owned in the 1800's by Gabriel Garbutt. The business thrived throughout the 19th century producing fire boiler bricks and sanitary products. Nearby was the community of 'Hole Bottom' including a row of cottages named the 'Five Houses', one of which was used as an Ale House, also owned by Garbutt and was named locally as 'The October Shop', the origin of that name I have failed to discover. The 'Shop' was frequented not only by workers from the nearby Bleachworks but also local miners. East of 'Hole Bottom' is a stile beyond which is a stream flowing to the south east. This is the beginning of Dean Brook. A steady climb from the stream, at the top of the hill is 'Scotsman's Stump'. An iron pillar erected in 1912 on which is a plaque, which reads '*In memory of George Henderson, Traveller, native of Annan, Dumfrieshire*', who it is said was barbarically murdered on Rivington Moor at noonday, November 9th, 1838. He had been shot in the head with a Black Powder Shotgun. He was taken to one of the five houses where he died of his wounds.

Figure 2 Scotsman's Stump erection 1912

Shortly after the tragedy a poem was written by A.E. Kirkman as a tribute to George Henderson.

A WINTERS TALE
BY A.E. KIRKMAN

Long ago I say on Winter Hill
A man was driven for to kill
An innocent Scots pedlar by name
of Henderson, of long held fame
Who has a Stump erected then
For reasons well beyond our ken
To-day still stands the Scotsman's Stump
The people who first erected it
Must certainly have had the hump
So shocked after the deadly deed
They quickly then did find need
To honour that poor wandering soul
Who ne'er alas, e'er reached his goal
But was cut down, and yet I say
The lust to kill lives on to-day

From the Stump the path continues to climb. To the right is the site of the long since demolished 'Ouzel Hall' a large building, the origins of which are extremely vague. It is said that a handloom weaver known locally as 'Owd Reynolds' built the Hall, which was described as a large cottage to accommodate his handlooms. He sold gingerbread and ale to wash it down, but he only sold the gingerbread, he gave the ale away to get round the licensing laws of the time. The cottage later became known as 'Newspaper Hall'. In the 19th century most people living on the moor could neither read nor write, but they were interested in the news from home and abroad, so someone who was reasonably literate would read out loud from the newspapers while the locals listened with interest, often debating between themselves about what they had heard. It is said that news of the Crimean War in 1854 fuelled a lengthy debate.

Most communities have their characters and the moor was no exception. Apart from Garbutt and Reynolds who could be described as entrepreneurs of their time, there were others who gained a reputation for shall we say, eccentricity. Such as Charlie 'Beawt Shirt' who was an old beggar who was often seen in the area around Coalpit Road and was so named, as one of the locals put it, **"If you gave him a shirt one day, to keep him warm, he would "be beawt" the next".** Another man of some repute was a character named Morris who owned a cottage known as 'Black Jacks'. He again sold gingerbread and ale to passing walkers. He had a reputation as a man with odd habits who it is said, threw a loaded pistol onto his cottage fire causing an explosion leaving the place an absolute shambles. He somehow survived unscathed.

Standing close to the highest point at approximately 1100 ft. is the Television Mast. The first mast was erected on the moor in 1948, originally for police communications. The Television Station was completed in 1957. There has been a number of incidents on the moor including several plane crashes. The most disastrous being in February, 1958, when a Silver City Airlines Bristol Wayfairer which on it's way to Manchester, carrying a party of motor dealers crashed on the summit very close to the T.V. mast. Thirty- five people lost their lives on that bleak, windswept moor, only seven survived. I remember that day vividly. At the time I lived on Johnson Fold just a few miles from the moor. Our neighbour, Bryn Thomas, a quietly spoken Welshman who was working at the T.V. Station was one of the first on the scene. Bryn described the devastation and horror he witnessed as he and his colleagues pulled survivors from the wreckage in driving snow.

It was time to move on. I took the path to the right and soon arrived at what remained of Burnt Edge Colliery. I sat by the fast flowing stream that soon becomes Dean Brook, the source of which is quarter of a mile to the east, as I had done with Grandpa nearly seventy years before. I took out a matchstick from the box, struck it and immediately put it out and as I sat alone with that little piece of wood in my hand, the memories came flooding back. If I put it in the 'Little River' would it, as he had said, **"Finish up in't Sea"**. I dropped it into the stream and thought will it? We'll find out as it disappeared from view. **"The matchstick's journey starts here".**

I was brought back to reality by the sound of dogs barking and was surrounded by four inquisitive Labradors followed by two women who greeted me with a friendly **"good morning".** After a brief chat they introduced themselves as Joan and Steph, mother and daughter who lived in one of the nearby converted farmhouses. During our conversation Joan was distracted, she looked to her left and said **"good morning Eddie",** I was a little bemused. I couldn't see anyone and then I saw a black net under a nearby hedgerow, from which came a cheery **"good morning".** Seeing the puzzled look on my face, Joan laughed and said **"that's Eddie, the Twitcher"** (Bird Watcher) **"he's here most days"** whereupon Eddie appeared from under the net holding his camera. The ladies went on their way followed by the dogs.   Eddie was quite excited telling me he had just discovered a family of quite rare 'Stone Chats' nesting close to the colliery site and had spent many hours 'watching them' as his family before him had done on these moors for generations. I left Eddie behind as it was time to follow the stream which tumbled into the valley below, taking the matchstick with it towards Walker Fold.

As I started to retrace my steps back down the causey path, I looked up to my left towards Coalpit Road, along which I had walked with my Grandpa, to reach this place on that unforgettable Saturday morning in 1946. Coalpit Road had been, for hundreds of years the main access from Halliwell onto the moor with it's farms, pits and quarries and was regularly used by the men who depended on these moors for their livelihood. However more recently, the area had become more popular with the ordinary people of Halliwell, who at weekends would enjoy walking over the moor to get away from the mills, factories and the confined spaces of terraced houses. They liked to 'get away' to the fresh air of the open countryside, most of which during the 19th century was owned by the Ainsworths of Smithills Hall, who had made a fortune in the 18th century from the West Indian Slave Trade. By the 19th century the Ainsworths had become one of the most prominent Bleachers in Lancashire, the profits from which enabled them in 1801 to purchase the Smithills Estate, including the Hall and Smithills Moor. By 1870 Richard Henry Ainsworth became Lord of the Manor at Smithills.

His favourite pastime was grouse shooting. He loved to take his friends on shooting expeditions on his land high above Bolton. He had a shooting hut built close to Coalpit Road, where he would take lunch with his friends. He became so possessive of his land that he decided to deny public access to the moor by closing Coalpit Road which passed through some of his favourite shooting land, thus denying the working man the enjoyment of walking freely over the moor as they had done for generations. In the Summer of 1896 a gate bearing the notice 'Trespassers will be prosecuted' was erected across the road near Holdens Farm and extra men were employed to stop public access. This action caused anger amongst the vast majority of the people of Bolton and in early September an advert was placed in the Bolton Journal and Guardian inviting the public to join a demonstration over Winter Hill Moor on Sunday, 6th September arranged by various organizations including the Bolton Socialist Party.

On that Sunday morning a crowd gathered outside the 'Waterloo' Pub at the junction of Halliwell Road and Blackburn Road and within a few minutes over 1,000 people led by a brass band set off up Halliwell Road soon to be joined by many others. They passed the rows of working class terraced houses bordering Halliwell Road, they weren't just from Halliwell but many other parts of the town. Many were employees of the Ainsworths, others were engineers and mill workers. They were also joined by colliers from the surrounding mining areas outside of Bolton. There were speeches by Political and Trade Union Leaders along the way. As the multitude passed the Ainsworth Arms and up the hill towards the gates of Smithills Hall it was estimated to be in excess of 10,000 people. On they walked, up the hill of Smithills Dean Road to Coalpit Road. Eventually they reached the disputed gate, where they were met by a small number of police and some of the Ainsworth gamekeepers. After some confusion, confrontation was inevitable, during which some of the police and Ainsworths men were injured. Re-enforcements were called from Halliwell Road Police Station but were not needed as order was restored and the crowd proceeded peacefully over the Moor towards Scotsman's Stump and Belmont. Their objective had been achieved and as the day wore on they returned to their homes.

There were minor demonstrations against the Ainsworths during the following months, including one on Winter Hill on Christmas day of 1896. However, after a long enquiry, during which various people gave good reason why they needed to use Coalpit Road, no real progress was made and the enthusiasm of both parties faded. Over 100 years later the people of Bolton enjoy total access to the moor and in June 1996, Bolton Council declared Coalpit Road a right of way.

Songs written to commemorate the trespass were popular at the time and were sung in Pubs across the town for many years. This one appeared in the Bolton Journal of 1896

O'er Winter Hill the people say
There's always been a right of way
Where working folk could go and look
On heathered Moor and rippling brook
But one good Christian now alas.
Says o'er this Moor yer must not pass
'Tis mine! but they hold array
Walked o'er and this to him did say -

That is all that survives of that Song

Another popular Song of the time runs as follows:-

Will you come o Sunday mornin
For a walk o'er Winter Hill
Ten thousand went last Sunday
But there's room for thousands still
O the Moors are rare and bonny
An the heathers sweet and fine
An the road across these hill tops
Is the public's - yours and mine

CHORUS -

So come on Sunday mornin
For a walk o'er Winter Hill
Ten thousand went last Sunday
But there's room for thousands still

O shame upon the Landlord
That would thrutch us up in town
Against such christless conduct
We will put our feet firm down
Ay we'll put our feet down strongly
Until we've clearly showed
Twenty thousand feet each Sunday
Can soon mark out a road!
Must poor folk stroll in cinders
While the rich cop all the green?
Is England's but the landlords?
Who locks up each pretty scene?
If they only could these tyrants
Would enclose the road to heaven!
So let us up and fight 'em
Even seventy times and seven!

CHORUS

So come on Sunday mornin - etc.

Both these songs reflect the feelings of the working man of Bolton at that time.

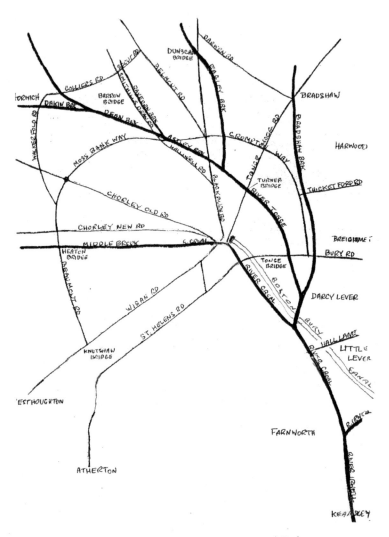

Map 2 Main roads & rivers around Bolton

After that period of reflection, I carried on walking down the 'Causey' and as I approached the signpost for Walker Fold Woods to my left, I looked and could see virtually the whole of Bolton in the distant valley. In the foreground was Barrow Bridge chimney a most recognizable landmark and I thought how many miners in the 19th century had walked down this path after a long shift underground on their way to their cottages in Colliers Row and Barrow Bridge and looked towards the town in the distance. The vista would have been dominated by numerous chimneys pouring out smoke polluting the whole valley.

Those chimneys belonged to the Mills, Engineering Factories and Bleachworks employing thousands of people across the town.

One such miner was Harry Gregory, a coal face worker at 'Burnt Edge' originally from Westhoughton, who in the late 1800's lived at 42 Colliers Row with his wife Catherine and their seven children, three sons and four daughters. It is likely that the children attended Colliers Row School, just along the road from their cottage. At that time 'Old Colliers Row' consisted of seven cottages occupied by miners and farm workers. They are appreciably older than 'New Colliers Row', adjoining the School and were probably built in the mid 1700's.

The School was built in 1841, funded by the Ainsworths and at approximately 800 ft. above sea level was the highest seat of learning in the Bolton Borough. It has four date stones, having been extended on three occasions, the first showing the date of construction, 1841. It was first extended in 1885 when a porch was added, then 13 years later in 1898 and again in 1900 when the present building was completed. The school was built to provide education for the children of Smithills Moor miners, hence the name, Colliers Row but also for the children of the quarrymen and the tenant farmers on the Smithills Estate. The school was a church school with the Vicar of St. Peter's officiating the Sunday service. It was also used as a 'Sunday School' for the children of the community.

During the late 1800's and early 1900's up to eighty children regularly attended the week day school. Excerpts from the school log in the late 1800's show how the inclement weather on the moor affected the attendance, for example, it is recorded that on the 24th March, 1898, there was an examination. The weather was so cold, the temperature in the classroom was 36 degrees 'F' and only one child attended. Even on the 8th of May of that year the records show *'no fire', wild and windy.* The school is feeling the effects of the severe weather. The only form of heating in the single classroom was an open coal fire and the record for 12th January, states *"The chimney was smoking badly and the room was filled with smoke"* The children were sent home. Now, in the mid 1900's the attendance is gradually falling.

I followed the signpost for Walker Fold Woods, turning left and leaving the causeway behind me, the path sloped gradually through the plantation to Dean Brook. I followed the flow of the brook towards Walker Fold. This valley is susceptible to flooding, as I was to discover in 1954. As a 16 year old I had just started work as an apprentice engineer at Hick Hargreaves in Bolton and lived on the Johnson Fold Council Estate, about one mile away. During that late summer my friends Johnny and David asked me if I would like to go camping with them. None of us had ever been camping before and had never even been in the Scouts, so our camping skills were non-existent, but I thought it would be an adventure living out in the open air. Johnny was the organizer. He had borrowed a four-man tent, primus stove and a frying pan, but none of us thought about a ground sheet. Our Mams had packed enough food to last us two days (we hoped), so on Friday evening, after tea, we set off carrying our rucksacks. Johnny carried the tent and off we went, across Old Links Golf Course, heading for Walker Fold with the intention of camping by 'Barrow Bridge River', as all the local kids knew the brook. We arrived at Walker Fold, climbed the fence and walked about quarter of a mile upstream and arrived at the grassy bank where I now stood. It was early evening, David and I started to erect the tent about six feet from the brook, while Johnny who considered himself to be a good cook lit a fire and soon had the primus stove going to prepare our evening meal. I asked **"What's for tea Johnny?"** he replied **"My speciality, "Pancakes", but first I'm brewing up"**. We got water from the brook and boiled it on the primus for a 'brew'. Everything was going smoothly and I thought, there's nothing to this camping. It was now about 9.00 p.m. and Johnny started to prepare our pancakes which with the luxury of sugar and lemon were a great success, so much so, that David and I were asking for more. After our meal, as darkness fell, we lay by the fire and played cards by the light of our bike lamps. As midnight approached it started to rain, so we decided it was time for sleep. We crawled into the tent and then realized we had no ground sheet, but we all had sleeping bags. I fell asleep to the sound of rain on the canvass and the brook flowing by. I awoke to the same sound at about 6.00 a.m. It was just about daylight. However, things felt a bit damp, in fact, more than damp, very wet. We soon realized the brook level had risen overnight and the tent was swamped. It didn't take us long, at 7.00 a.m. to pack up and go home. We walked home in torrential rain eating Mam's homemade buttered flatcake (which she had made the previous day) for breakfast. We arrived home one hour later, absolutely saturated after one night in the great outdoors. No more camping for me.

Figure 3 The "Cigarette Tunnel"

As I turned towards my next objective, that memory of my youth made me smile - just a little! After a steady, if undulating walk along the bank of the brook, I was soon approaching the 'cigarette tunnel', so named by generations of local kids since the late 1800's when cigarettes became popular. It is no more than a tubular culvert through which Dean Brook flows under Walker Fold Road. The matchstick would gather speed as the flow of the brook increases as it reaches the narrow entrance to the tunnel. In 1805 an Act of Parliament was secured for a new turnpike road joining the Bolton to Blackburn highway from Scout Road, passing Colliers Row, to join the little Bolton to Chorley turnpike from Doffcocker at Old Kiln Lane and the

'Bob's Smithy Inn'. This became Walker Fold Road, completed in 1806.

During the long summer holidays of the 1950's the tunnel was a popular playground for the kids of Johnson Fold, only twenty minutes away across the Old Links Golf Course. Depending on the level of water flowing through the tunnel we would run through it and jump into the rock pool at the outlet. Climb back up the hill to the road, cross over, down the other side and run through the tunnel again. A great game. The brook exits the tunnel into a large rock pool surrounded by a grassed area, an ideal playground and a popular picnic spot.

It is at this point where the surrounding landscape starts to change. From the rugged moorland of Winter Hill in the west to the lush, tree covered valley of Halliwell Glen. The brook cascades over rocks probably laid down by glacial activity thousands of years ago, creating the glen, formerly known as High Shores Clough, into what is, the most picturesque section of the match's journey to Barrow Bridge, just a few hundred yards downstream. We spent many happy hours in the 1950's playing, jumping from rock to rock along this beautiful river valley, which could now be submerged under many feet of water. When in the1880's a proposal by Parliament that many of Bolton's townships should have a new, better water supply from a reservoir, which would be created by damming Dean

Brook and Dakins Brook, the two brooks became one below the 63 Steps. At this point three township borders meet, to the west of the steps is the Halliwell township, to the east is Heaton and in the centre the steps are in Horwich township. The Dam would be built here and the dip in the land above the cigarette tunnel would be raised to make Walker Fold Road approximately fifty-five feet higher by building another Dam beneath the road. The whole scheme would create a reservoir stretching from Barrow Bridge in the east, up to Burnt Edge in the west. However, Col. R.H. Ainsworth of Smithills Hall was opposed to the scheme. He contended that his Bleachworks, although well downstream from the proposed Dam, used the waters of Dean Brook in the bleaching process and he highlighted the fact that if the Dam was ever breached, his Bleachworks and all lower Halliwell and Astley Bridge would be flooded. Ainsworth and his allies were successful in their opposition and the scheme was shelved.

A record of the Bolton Field Naturalists Saturday Walk appeared in the Bolton Evening News on October 1st, 1912. It read's

'Forty members took part on Saturday in a very enjoyable ramble over the moors under the leadership of Mr. Openshaw and one of the keepers from Smithills Estate, meeting at the Halliwell Tramcar Terminus. The party proceeded to Barrow

Bridge and from that place they entered the High Shore Glen, which well deserves the name given to it, for it has all the characteristics of a glen such as few people of our town would imagine the district possessed. As the party proceeded, many specimens were gathered, although it is rather late in the year for flowers, and these were named and explained by the Botanical Secretary. After passing through the glen they then went along Dean Brook and on the left could be seen Burnt Edge, and looking at this from a distance in the valley, the name seems quite appropriate. It looks as if there has been a fire all along the side of the hill, blackening it for a quarter of a mile. On the right could be seen Sugar Loaf Hill, which some seem to think is an artificial hill, it having been an ancient burial ground, although others seem to have quite a different opinion on the matter'.

'We begged to differ and continued our walk over the moor'.

Dean Brook and the matchstick have now reached the point where it is joined by Dakins Brook, from the right. Also to the right are the 63 steps built into the side of the hill overlooking the brook. At the top of the steps, to the left are the remains of a building. This was originally Twitchell's Farm owned during most of the 1800's by Robert Eatock, who around 1795 realized that Barrow Bridge had hundreds of people working in the local mill plus miners and quarrymen working on Smithills Moor.

The village had no Pub, so Eatock decided, first to convert the farm into a Beer House, which he
called the 'Brown Cow', which kept the locals in beer for the next sixty years. He also realized that all these people had to climb a very steep hill to get to his Pub so, to make access easier he had the steps built.

Figure 4 Twitchells

On the left, across the brook from the steps is a flat area of grassland. This is the site of 'Carding Mill' the first Mill to be built in this valley in the 1700's by Robert Whewell. The Mill was driven by a water wheel powered by the fast flowing brook. The Mill thrived and was soon attracting workers from as far afield as Horwich. In 1795 he sold the Mill to Robert and John Lord, the sons of Robert Lord of Lord's Fold at Doffcocker, who had a well established three Storey Mill at Lower Heys, which stood approximately where Johnson Fold Primary School stands to-day and was demolished during the construction of Moss Bank Way in the mid 1930's. The Lord brothers, like their father were very shrewd businessmen and as 'Carding Mill' continued to prosper, they decided to build a new much more modern Mill further down the brook, around which the village as we know it to-day developed and which I will describe later. The brook continues to flow east over the weir, constructed by the Lords in the early 1800's. The matchstick negotiates the weir and now approaches the bridge, over which is Longshaw Ford Lane, an ancient pack horse way, dating back hundreds of years which led from Darwen in the north to Wigan and Warrington in the South.

This was used by cattle drovers and traders who passed through here moving livestock and merchandise from market to market. From this point the pack road, which still exists to-day, carried on over what is now 'The Old Links' Golf Course, passing the 'Striking Ass' a hostelry later known as 'T Kickin' Donkey where the packmen could rest, eat and drink. The road continues west, emerging close to the 'Bob's Smithy' Pub and on down Old Kiln Lane.

Longshaw Ford Lane brings back happy memories for me. I recall a day in September, 1957. I was nineteen years old, it was the day I bought my first car, a 1936 B.S.A. "V" Twin Three Wheeler. I had paid a workmate £15 for it. I brought it home to our house on Johnson Fold Estate and when my Dad saw it, he said **"What's that Al"**, (he always called me 'Al') **"It looks like a green coffin on wheels"** and smiled as he saw the registration number COF 607. **"I'll be your first passenger, let's go to Barrow Bridge".** The journey only took a few minutes and as we passed the boating lake to our left Dad said **"It runs well Al, I'll bet you two bob (ten pence) it won't go up Longshaw Ford Lane to Colliers Row",** not realizing the car had been a competition 'Hill Climber'. Needless to say Dad lost his 'Two Bob'. I did a lot of 'courtin' in that car over the following couple of years and sold it, at a profit for £20.

This beautiful part of our town brings back so many happy memories of that long summer school holiday of 1952. The first year of life on the newly built Johnson Fold Estate, situated only half a mile away across the golf course. We spent most days, weather permitting playing on the hills overlooking the village, occasionally venturing down to the 'Penny Slot Hut' by the boating lake. As I continued my walk, those hills were to my right. To my left are the famous houses fronting Dean Brook, each with it's own individual footbridge across the brook. These were built in the 1830's for the Managers and

Over-lookers of the huge Dean Mills, built further down the road. I recall during that period, these houses served cream teas in their front gardens to the hundreds of visitors to the village, arriving on the No. 4 bus from Bolton and the surrounding districts. I distinctly remember one of the houses had a 'Hovis' sign hanging by the door. As I approached the entrance to the boating lake area, I noticed two stone pillars, which had obviously been gateposts and the gate that was once between them was the entrance to 'Clough Houses'. There were originally six houses built in the 1800's to house the workers at Dean Mills. No photographs seem to exist of 'Clough Houses' but the roofs can be seen on old photographs of the adjacent boating lake and the tea rooms. The houses which were some of the oldest in the village were demolished in the 1920's. Directly after the gate posts is the site of what was once the main attraction of the village, the boating lake. This was originally built in 1836 as a reservoir, supplying water to Ainsworths Bleachworks further down Dean brook and first opened as a boating lake in 1905. Standing beside the lake were the Victorian timber buildings. One was the tearoom and the other housed a number of 'Penny Slot' machines, which some lads (not from Johnson Fold) armed with a penknife, found it relatively easy to remove the pennies from the machines to spend in the local shop.

Figure 5 Barrow Bridge Lake

Figure 6 Slot Machine hut in the background

Figure 7 Barrow Bridge shop

As I left the lake, directly opposite is another ancient stone footbridge spanning the brook. From here a track climbing steeply to a point overlooking the village leads to Smithills Dean Road and Smithills Hall, passing Pendlebury's Farm.

A sluice was built to divert water from the brook into the reservoir which later became the boating lake. From here the flow of the brook and the matchstick gather pace towards the waterfall, built during the straightening of the brook to improve the flow of water to the mill. On the opposite side of the brook and accessed by another stone footbridge are four cottages, built around 1800 to house mill workers. The end cottage No. 61, with a substantial plot of land was owned for sixty years by the Chapel family. They were market gardeners and their greenhouses and vegetable gardens covered most of the area on the opposite side of the brook above the waterfall. To my right, opposite the footbridge is another row of cottages which I vividly remember on our visits to the village in the 1940' having their doors open with small vases containing a single rose for sale for 'Gentlemen's Button Holes'. The last building in the row is the village shop, originally the Dean mill workers Co-operative shop, where, in the late 1940's during our regular visits to Barrow Bridge, I spent my bus fare home on a liquorice root and walked home to Brownlow Fold chewing it. Built into the wall of the shop, is the oldest surviving post box in Bolton, dating from the days of the modern postal system, installed in the 1840's, bearing the royal cipher 'V.R' Victoria Regina and still in use to-day.

Directly across Barrow Bridge Road formerly known as Mill Street and again accessed by a footbridge across the brook is the Barrow Bridge Mission, which is the only surviving part of the adjoining Dean Mills. This was the Mill Repair Workshop, later to become a cafe and in 1930 a Mission Church. Another shop, on the right was famous for it's ice cream, but as kids we could never afford it. I do recall there being a Victorian weighing machine, which was chained to the wall outside the shop. The last building in the village, on the right is 'Mill House', built for the Lord brothers Mill Manager, later occupied by their younger brother Peter.' The cottage is still there and is now 'Dean Mill Cottage'. Directly opposite the cottage and shops is an area of woodland. This is the site of the original Dean Mill, built by the Lord brothers in 1800 and powered by a forty two feet waterwheel using the fast flowing waters of the brook. This was the seed from which the Barrow Bridge community grew. The mill thrived for some years, but the Lord brothers overstretched themselves financially, incurring massive debts and eventually, in 1816 they were forced into bankruptcy. The mills then became under the control of Richard Ainsworth who owned the land on which the mill was built, who, along with others allowed the firm to go back into business under the name of Lord and Noble, directly managed by Peter Lord. The business seemed to flourish for some years, but by 1830 the firm was again in financial trouble and in 1835 it was put up for auction. It was then purchased by Gardner and Bazley who not only built a new mill on the site but, in 1835 completely transformed the whole Dean Brook valley all the way up to Langshaw Ford Bridge. This completely changed the course of the brook and by moving the reservoir used by the Lords to the other side of the brook, created a new reservoir, later to become the famous boating lake. This would be used along with various smaller lodges and sluices to feed water into the brook during periods of drought.

A new, up to date mill was built, described in 1851 as the largest Cotton Company in Britain. The new mill used steam power and any water needed was sourced from the brook. The new mill consisted of two six storey buildings, each with it's own 150 ft. chimney between which was the engine house. A canteen was built for the employees.

A large area of land to the south of the mill owned by the Barrows family, from which the name Barrow Bridge derives, was purchased and a totally new purpose built village was constructed to house the workforce. Five rows of back to back cottages were built, along with a further three rows of three storey houses. Each house had running water supplied by a newly built reservoir fed by Hollin Hey Stream. Access to the village was via the 'Long Steps' from Barrow Bridge Road to Bazley Street, named after Sir Thomas Bazley and the five rows of cottages joining it were simply named, First, Second, Third, Fourth and Fifth Street. To the left, at the top of the steps, is the village Institute designed and built, along with the rest of the village in 1846 by Bazley for the education and entertainment of his employees. He was also instrumental in the development of the original track leading past Clough Houses to Langshaw Ford, including building the houses, with the individual foot bridges on the north side of the brook. These houses were built to house the Mill Managers. The bridges, as we know them to-day were built some time later.

On Saturday, 11th October, 1852, Prince Albert, Queen Victoria's Consort, visited the Dean Mills Estate. He had been so impressed when he saw the Dean Mills exhibits at the Great Exhibition of 1851, he was determined to visit the village and the impressive mill. After the historic visit the whole workforce attended a fine 'Do' at the Institute, being waited on by the Mill Managers and their wives. The prince was so impressed with what he saw that Bazley later became Sir Thomas Bazley.

Figure 8 Barrow Bridge Mills

In 1862 the mills and the rest of the estate were sold for £100,000 to the Callender family who continued production until the mills finally closed in 1877.

Following the closure, the village gradually declined and became known as the 'Deserted Village' and Albert Haggas Bryan Halliwell's famous historian, writing in the Bolton Standard in 1959 quotes

'Scenes reminiscent of the darkest days of the cotton famine now returned, hungry faces, smokeless chimneys, silent mills. The blow was mortal, desolation stalked the streets, the houses fell into ruins and the place literally became a deserted village'.

In 1893, local writer, Allen Clarke, otherwise known as 'Teddy Ashton' wrote in his book 'Tales of a deserted village' He writes

'I remember Barrow Bridge when it really was a deserted village, only one of the cottages by the brook was tenanted. When all the houses upon the village green and the Institute were empty with rotting windows and doors, the grass growing on the doorsteps. When the bleak, bare walls stood like great skeletons, surveying a scene of desolation and decay'.

DESERTED VILLAGE
BY FRED PLANT

The following article first appeared in the London Morning Leader on the 17th May, 1901.

It was re-printed in the form of a small booklet together with some photographs and advertisements and sold for one penny.

It is reproduced here exactly as it was written originally.

'Over the edge of the earthy basin wherein lies Bolton, Lancashire, at the foot of the moors which stretch away in wild undulating grandeur to the north west of that smoke hung basin, lies Barrow Bridge, Lancashire's 'Deserted Village'. The Millbank of Disraeli's 'Coningsby', but it is no longer the model village the tip top, regular, slap up place Coningsby was advised to go and inspect. That is from an industrial point of view. The industrial ideal, like the utilitarian eye, is a wavering thing at the best, and appeals not to your true lover of nature'.

THE SILENT MILLS

'I am sitting on a grassy slope overlooking Barrow Bridge. At my feet, gaunt and grim, like serried, sightless monsters that have been killed standing and had their vitals drawn, I see the

remnants of the two mills that used to groan and hum with human toil, limbs and brains obeying steam and iron.

That was 25 years ago. To-day I hear the piping of a bird that hops along the low wall in front of the low building from whence, in departed days, came the thud, thud of powerful engines, the tinkle of a waterfall and the lowing of kine waft onward on a kissing breeze. All else is mute'.

THE COTTAGES

'To my left, as I sit on the crest of the hill facing the silent mills, a clump of cottages, built in back to back style, with strips of garden in front, represent the one time domestic nest of the mill workers. They were built for the operatives within sound of the turreted bell over the engine house. The cottages are inhabited now but in many cases the inmates are expected to respond to either a bell or a buzzer in the town, nearly three miles away. Most of the inhabitants though, eke out a living by supplying teas and refreshments to visitors. Ten years ago there were but two families left in the village and the stone cottages, like the mills were deserted. In the narrow streets the grass grew several feet high and human foot rarely trod the bye-paths. Whilst the deserted state of the village was 'discovered' by the Salvation Army and it was freely rumoured that General Booth had all but settled to carry out his 'Darkest England' scheme within it's precincts, negotiations fell through and the grass continued to grow over the paths where the clang of hurrying clogs had once been. *This refers to an attempt by the Salvation Army to take over the village, which never materialized'.*

The deserted village inspired so many literary minds to put pen to paper during the late 1800's and in 1903 Allen Clarke, lover of Bolton's countryside and especially Barrow Bridge wrote a poem called

SWEET SUNSET OVER BARROW BRIDGE

Sweet sunset over Barrow Bridge
The daylight fades over moorland ridge
The white farms on green slopes go dim
The throstle sings his goodnight hymn
While in the western sky afar
Rises the golden evening star
Oe'r meadow path and greystone walls
The glamour of the twilight falls

So er'e the drowsy night come down
The children all trudge back to town
Tired with their fun in the fresh air
where grass is good and wild flowers fair
The games are done the races run
The pleasure and prizes won
O'er skipping ropes and bats and balls
The sleep charm of the twilight falls

The moon looks over rustling trees
Which murmer low like gentle seas
The swallows now have ceased to gleam
Athwart the beauty of the stream
In gladsome peace the glad day ends
For young and old for lovers, friends
O'er hills and valleys, hamlets, halls,
The blessing of the twilight falls

ALLEN CLARKE - 1903

A.V. Webster, a writer from London visited Barrow Bridge in the early 1900's before the mills were demolished and had not operated for 30 years. He was moved to write :-

GAUNT MILLS THAT SEEM SADLY FADING

Examplars of grief in stone
The visitor stands upbraiding, where utterly left alone
Behold we have heard the spindle awhirrin in seasons past
Who now list to the leaping rindle and the moorland blast

The bell in the turrets broken, unfit for a ghastly clang
Though partly a tyrants taken, it's dumbness provokes a pang
We once heard its loud peel ringing to work as it did play
What a thrill would its voice be bringing did it ring to-day

A.V. WEBSTER

When in 1897, Thomas Heydock bought the old Institute Building and opened his Barrow Bridge Laundry, several of his employees rented some of the cottages off Bazley Street and made them habitable once more. Other people came, possibly inspired by Allen Clarke's stories of the village, but more likely, some of the derelict cottages could be rented for as little as half a crown (two shillings and six pence) a week. In subsequent years there was also an influx of people looking for somewhere to live after the First World War when there was a shortage of housing. The mills were demolished in 1913. All that remained of them was the Archway that led to the Engine House. The archway was known locally as 'Marble Arch' until it too was demolished in the 1920's. The area became the No. 4 Bus Terminus, again accessed by a bridge over the brook.

To quote the late Derek Billington and Clive Walsh from their book 'Barrow Bridge' -:

'The village ends here amongst the houses built by two men who over 150 years ago realized their dream of building a model village for their employees'.

The village still survives to-day.

Figure 9 Marble Arch

I walked across the road to the bus terminus and looked over the handrail to the brook below, meandering to the east towards the matchstick's next objective, Victoria Lake, and I'm sure I caught a glimpse of it floating by. As I looked at the surface of the brook I noticed that it was exceptionally shallow and that the bed of the brook appeared wide and flat which wasn't natural and that this section seemed to have had extensive work done. After some enquiries, I discovered that in the 1940's, Barrow Bridge, near the village shop was flooded several times after periods of heavy rain. After investigation by borough engineers they concluded that the major cause of the flooding was too much debris, boulders, rocks etc. on the bed of Dean Brook restricting the flow of water, hence the severe flooding. All these obstructions were removed and the bed of the brook was levelled thus relieving the build -up of water.

It was time to move on. At this point I had two alternatives, do I take the footpath to the left of the brook and follow it to Victoria Lake, or do I take the road to the right? I decided to follow the road first and return to the brook later. I walked past, to my right, the 'Long Steps' leading up to the model village and onto, again on my right, 'Cinder Lane' which I followed, up the hill, shortly arriving at 'Lightbounds' to my left. This is an imposing building which is recognized as one of oldest houses in the Halliwell township, built by the Lightbowns (note the slight difference in the early spelling) in the mid 1600's, probably as a farm. During the Civil War the Lightbowns were staunch parliamentarians and during that period parliamentary soldiers were billeted at Lightbounds. In fact, it is recorded that three of the family were slain during the Siege of Bolton in 1644.

To my right is Stannings Lodge, a natural oasis of shrubs and trees surrounding a picturesque lake. Stannings, was used, in the 1840's as a source of fresh water piped to the newly constructed Dean Mills Model Village. The lodge was named after John Stanning a close friend of John Horrocks Ainsworth the man responsible for the success and prosperity of Ainsworth's bleachworks. The history of which I will cover later. During his later years he had very poor eyesight and needed help and support. He got this from Stanning, a close friend who had worked for the Ainsworths for many years and John Horrocks trusted him implicitly.

In 1959, writing in the Bolton Standard, Albert Haggas Bryan, the well-known local historian, describes the difficulties. Ainsworth, in 1860, was virtually blind. Bryan quotes:- *'Alas the owner of it all could not see'.* By this time Mr. Ainsworth was totally blind. We can picture him leaning on the arm of his friend, John Stanning, perambulating his extensive works, avoiding machinery and feeling with his sensitive fingers, the finish of the cloth. Despite his affliction he remained assiduous in business.

I turn left into Swallowfield Lane, down the hill towards Moss Bank. To my right is the entrance to the locally famous 'Rock Gardens' opened in 1928, a place that has given pleasure over the years, to thousands of Bolton folk for generations, including my family and I. It was here along with my friends from Johnson Fold that I played war games amongst the rocks and foliage in the early 1950's.

I walked just a few yards further and again to my right stands a substantial stone building dated 1853. This was originally the stables for the working horses of the Moss Bank Estate.

I turn left. I am now at what was the rear entrance to Moss Bank House, the family home of two generations of the Ainsworth family.

In 1748, Peter Ainsworth, of the bleaching family, took out a lease on Lightbounds and spent most of his life in the house, which still overlooks Moss Bank. Peter and his son Richard were intent on developing the Lightbounds Estate and around

1790 they acquired both the 'Lumwood' and the 'Hunts' Estates which adjoined Lightbounds. Peter had big plans for this land. He envisaged building a great house on what had been called 'The Moss' as a dwelling for Richard, his wife Sarah and their family. He called it 'Moss Bank'. Peter Ainsworth himself never lived there, preferring to live the rest of his life at his beloved 'Lightbounds'. Local journalist 'A Haggas Bryan' who took a keen interest in the Ainsworths, observed *'We can visualize the old bleacher gazing through the window of Lightbounds as Moss Bank House gradually grew. We can imagine his exultation at this palpable evidence of the rise of the Ainsworths'.*

Figure 10 Moss Bank House from a drawing by Peter Nightingale

Moss Bank house was completed in 1795. The house was an imposing building, four storeys high and possessing 37 windows on the south front alone. It was built with top quality, local handmade bricks. In all, including offices and servant's quarters, nearly 100 windows were counted. There was a comprehensive library, containing hundreds of books, some extremely valuable. The whole house was furnished with high quality pieces of furniture and fine paintings adorned the walls. All in all, a home of exceptional opulence, reflecting the wealth of the Ainsworths at that time.

Joseph Kefford, the head gardener, had designed lawns, conservatories, fountains, a circular fish pond and a high walled kitchen garden, which still exists as the high walled Rose Garden. There was a large cobbled area at the rear of the house, comprising domestic offices, stables, coach house and kennels. On a hill above these buildings was an elaborate terrace and aviary with peach and vine houses on the sunny south slope. It is here that the detached tower which John Horrocks Ainsworth used for his favourite pastime astronomy, stood. The tower which housed his telescope still stands to-day with its ornate Victorian windows. The tower also housed a kitchen with domestic quarters. I vaguely remember in the late 1940's the house, the mounting stone by the stables for lady riders, the watering trough and the stable yard arch.

No Victorian country house of status would be without it's 'Ice House' and Moss Bank was no exception. The 'Ice House' was, as the name suggests the Victorian, 'Deep Freeze'. This is where all the everyday produce, such as game, fresh meat, vegetables, dairy produce and above all the Ainsworth's substantial collection of vintage wines was stored. It was located some fifteen feet underground, in close proximity to the main house and accessed by a flight of stone steps into a brick lined chamber measuring approximately twelve feet by six feet. The structure was topped with a domed glass roof protruding just above ground level giving some light to the room below.

In the early 1800's, to further enhance the south facing aspect of the house, Richard Ainsworth, a man of vision, realized that Hollin Hey Brook, running from it's source high above Moss Bank and adjacent to the Estate was an unused asset, not only to the appearance of the house, but also as a valuable source of water for his thriving bleaching business. Hollin Hey stream was diverted into a prepared 'Cut' or canal through the estate, passing the front of the house and on to the bleachworks where it drained into Dean Brook. The canal was one of the distinctive features of the Moss Bank landscape. the other was the rock gardens. Built much later.

In 1870, the Ainsworths left Moss Bank and moved to Smithills Hall. The house was let to William Hargreaves of Hick Hargreaves & Co. Ltd., who lived at Moss Bank for several years, after which the house was partly used by two elderly spinsters, the Misses Rosetti and Richardson, until 1900, when the Bleachers Association used it as offices until 1928. The house and gardens were then sold to Bolton Corporation, who officially opened Moss Bank Park on 27th June, 1928. For the next twenty years parts of the house were put to various uses.

During World War Two, it was used as the headquarters for the 'Home Guard'. By 1949 the old house had fallen into disrepair and Bolton Corporation reluctantly decided it should be demolished, which was carried out in 1951 and the area was grassed over.

I walked on past the site of the old stables and kennels with the walled Rose Garden to my right and a Cart House to my left. I carried on down the slope and paused to admire the view. This is the view the Ainsworths would have admired from the windows of Moss Bank House. I remember, as a lad, the canal or 'Cut' as the Ainsworths called it, flowed under the bridge in the direction of the bleachworks site. To my left the path follows the line of the old water course towards the Amphitheatre. The path then leads over the hill, behind the old bleachworks site, down a grassy slope to join Barrow Bridge Road, close to the access to Victoria lake, which I will visit later. I then walked back, past 'Cinder Lane' and down the hill to the old number 4 Barrow Bridge bus terminus.

I had come full circle.

It was time to resume my walk along the footpath by Dean Brook from the bus terminus, heading towards the matchsticks next objective, Victoria Lake. To my left is a large area of woodland. This was the site of Dean Mills, which faced the brook for a distance of approximately 200 metres. As I followed the path with the brook to my right, it was noticeable that this stretch of water had been re-routed and considerable work had been done. Not only to the bed of the brook, where all obstructions to the flow had been removed, but rocks had been placed uniformly along its banks. Obvious evidence of the work carried out in the 1940's to prevent further flooding of Barrow Bridge. I was now approaching the lake. I came to a gate with a notice advising 'Private Land', so I could go no further along this path. I could see the lake through the trees. I decided to retrace my steps back to the bus terminus and approach the lake from the opposite side at a later date.

From the bus terminus I followed the road towards the 'Big Chimney', standing on the site of 'Ainsworths Bleachworks' which, in the 1800's was recognized as the leading bleaching concern in the Country. They were by far the largest employer in the area, employing hundreds of people in the Halliwell township. The Company was founded by Peter Ainsworth, who became known as Peter of the Moss. He was born in 1713 and by 1740, at the age of twenty seven he had established his bleaching business at Lower Pools using the 'Grassing' method of bleaching which is simply stretching the woven cloth on frames left in the sun to bleach naturally. His business soon started to grow and as early as 1741 he had taken on apprentices described in the township records of the period as 'Paupers Sons' (James Haddock's son and John Morris's lad). The business continued to prosper and around 1770 his son Peter, further expanded the business being an even more astute businessman than his father. Peter senior died in 1780, by which time Peter junior had expanded the business even further. By 1785 bleaching was moving from an outdoor based business to an indoor one, so in the late 1780's Peter Ainsworth, who by now had been joined in the business by his son Richard, acquired a substantial area of land to the east of Moss Bank from Captain Dewhurst of Halliwell Hall, who, at the time was the areas major landowner. The Bleachworks grew rapidly and by 1790, Peter Ainsworth became known as 'The Opulent Bleacher', because of his phenomenal wealth, and in 1801 the Ainsworths purchased the Smithills Estate, including Smithills Hall for a mere £21,000. It was intended as an ancestral home for future generations of the family.

The Hall had been neglected for many years and much time and money was spent bringing it back to it's former glory. Following Richard's death in 1833, his fourth son, John Horrocks Ainsworth of Moss Bank continued to run the business. He had also gained a reputation as a Builder and was responsible for the funding and building of a number of local churches and schools. However, he was beset by problems, his eyesight was gradually deteriorating and in his later years, even though virtually blind he was an efficient and enthusiastic employer. During this period, in the mid 1800's the croft was at it's busiest and during this time it increased in size dramatically as new extensions were built and alterations made to generate an increase in production.   The stone used to extend the Bleachworks and for building some cottages provided for senior employees, came from the Ainsworths own quarry on the Smithills Estate, even the coal used to fire the furnaces was mined from Smithills own Pit employing up to fifty miners producing an average of 50 tons of coal a day.

The mid to late 1800's was a period of stability for the Bleachworks. However, on the 1st April, 1865, John Horrocks died and in the south transept of St. Peter's, Halliwell, one of the churches he funded and helped build, there is a marble tablet to his memory. It reads:-

'In memory of John Horrocks Ainsworth of Moss Bank, this memorial is erected by his workpeople employed by him in testimony of their grateful remembrance of his unwearied interest and of his consistent liberality in promoting it. Born 18th August, 1800. Died 1st April, 1865.

After the death of John Horrocks, Richard Henry Ainsworth became, not just the new owner of the Bleachworks, but one of the largest landowners in the town. However, he was not a bleacher, as his predecessors had been and needed help to run the business. He turned to John Stanning, who had been John Horrocks's confident and works manager during most of the mid 1800's which had been the Bleachworks most profitable period. He made Stanning a partner in the business, but after only a few months, because of the Colonel's lack of business knowledge, they could not agree on several counts and the partnership was dissolved by mutual agreement, within a year of John Horrocks' death.

The business continued for some years but the Colonel did not have the drive and enthusiasm of John Horrocks, having had the benefit of an education at one of the country's premier schools, Eton. From Eton he went on to Christchurch, Oxford and from thence into the family business. He commanded respect from his employees and did not have the same relationship with them as his predecessor had.

In the 1870's Annabel Huth Jackson, Richard Ainsworth's cousin, in her Memoirs *'A Victorian Childhood'* writes, *'When the holidays came, we went to Smithills Hall, my cousin Richard's real home, then to the bleaching works, a family business in which every man, woman and child had grown up serving the Ainsworths. It was a great joy to us and we were always wandering round, watching the processes and inhaling the pungent odours of the bleachworks, which we as children honestly liked, a strange taste'.* The mills hands, some of whom had worked for the Ainsworths most of their lives, were almost part of the family. Old men would say, **"Ah, your't daughter of Julia, who wer't daughter o' Hannah, who wer't daughter O' owd Mr. Ainsworth up at th'All".** The family were only remembered by their Christian names. Class distinction still prevailed with the 'Colonel' There was always an arrogance about him and as the years went by into the 1900's he was losing interest in the running of the Bleachworks. Nevertheless, he still took the occasional walk through the rucks and stillages of the Croft. Some of the older crofters gave him the nickname 'Owd Dick'. On his strolls round the Croft, he usually took his dogs with him. The dogs were greeted with mixed feelings by the workforce. They ran in front of the Colonel and gave warning of 'Owd Dick's' approach.

In the early 1900's, Richard Ainsworth sold the Bleachworks to the 'Bleachers Association' which carried on production in the 'Capital Works' (which I will visit later) until 1925 when production transferred to the 'Prospect' works in Croft Road. This finally closed in 1931. The end of an era.

Over subsequent years most of the Bleachworks buildings were put to various uses. I will visit these buildings as I walk through the site. 'The Big Chimney' is the first substantial structure on the Bleachworks site. As I approach it from Barrow Bridge, directly below the chimney, on my left and standing on a sharp bend in the road is 'Croft Cottage'. This was originally the Bleachworks Shop, or the 'Tuck Shop' as the workers knew it, supplying a wide range of provisions and foodstuffs for hungry mouths. Towering above the cottage is 'Barrow Bridge Chimney' one of Bolton's most famous landmarks, but not actually in Barrow Bridge, which is approximately a quarter of a mile away. Built in 1863 and probably the last major project that John Horrocks Ainsworth was directly involved with just two years before his death. For some time he felt that the existing chimneys of the Bleachworks were too small and thought a larger chimney, built on higher ground would disperse the fumes and pollution generated by the Bleachworks boilers, thus avoiding damage to the cloth being bleached.

When completed the chimney stood three hundred and six feet high, but was reduced in 1924 to two hundred and eighty eight feet. It has since been reduced again to it's present height of two hundred and forty six feet. During its construction a system of ropes and pulleys was devised to hoist the building materials up the chimney. Ropes were attached to a harnessed team of horses travelling along what is now Moss Lane. They could heave the necessary bricks and mortar up to the appropriate level for the bricklayers to lay the thousands of bricks. At the 'Topping Out' ceremony local dignitaries were hoisted to the top of the chimney in a large basket to celebrate with a 'Tea Party' at three hundred feet above the bleachworks. On completion it was recognized as the tallest chimney in Lancashire.

Until comparatively recently a lead plate was affixed to the base of the stack bearing the initials 'J.H.A.', for John Horrocks Ainsworth and the date 1863. Unfortunately, it has been removed, possibly by a souvenir hunter.

Figure 11 Artist's impression of "Thunderbird House"

As recently as October, 2011, it was reported in the 'Bolton News' that despite numerous objections, plans for an innovative home dubbed the 'Thunderbird House', because of it's similarity to a house in a 1960's Children's T.V. series. It was for a two storey, four bedroom, two bathroom, glass fronted house, built around the chimney approximately sixty feet above ground level with panoramic views over Moss Bank Park and the surrounding moorland. The plan was approved, but the 'Thunderbird House' was never built.

John Horrocks Ainsworth, would have 'turned in his grave' at the thought of his ultimate achievement, a landmark of which he was extremely proud being disfigured in such a way. In fact, the question was once asked why did such an astute businessman establish a mansion (Moss Bank House) with his tall works chimney staring into his drawing room window? The cynics at the time offered one answer, the same astute Victorian businessman liked to keep an eye on his chimney, even from the luxury of his drawing room. If the smoke ribbon rising from it was long and vigorous, there was work and wealth afoot for his Bleachworks.

Opposite the chimney, to my right is the site of 'The Capital Works' comprising a number of buildings and recreational facilities for the Ainsworths employees. 'The Capital Works' was the site of the original 'Holy Well' so named after St. Catherine of Sienna, from which Halliwell takes it's name. Tradition, which is often right, records that the 'Holy Well' stood on this site as early as the 14th century and was much frequented by travellers to partake of the healing waters. However, in 1744, the three year old daughter of Peter Ainsworth, who by this time owned the land, fell into the Well and drowned, after which Ainsworth ordered the Well to be filled in. Over one hundred years later in 1849 the Well was re-discovered by John Horrocks Ainsworth who diverted the waters from the well stream, through a tunnel to feed Dean Brook where it emerged as 'Holy Well Spring identified by a decorative stone arch dated

1849. This still exists, but is virtually inaccessible, because of the dense vegetation surrounding it. The original spring no longer exists.

Figure 12 Halliwell Bleachworks

Standing next to the 'Holy Well' site is the 'The Old Fire Station', in which was kept the Ainsworths own Fire Engine, an earlier one was hauled and operated by the crew. Later John Horrocks replaced it with a horse drawn appliance named the 'Queen Anne', complete with leather buckets and ladders, manned by a four man team.

Figure 13 Ainsworth's Fire Brigade

Many of the horses used to pull the company's fleet of carts were kept in the adjoining stables. Every day five teams, two teams of three horses each and three teams of two horses, set off from the works at 2.00 a.m. to make the journey to Manchester. The journey could sometimes take up to six hours. At any one time there could have been up to one hundred horses stabled there. These horses were a valuable asset to the company and were extremely well looked after by experienced stable lads who were led by the head horseman, Sam Walls, who had been employed by the Ainsworths for many years. He lived nearby with his wife, cat and dog in an old multi coloured, gypsy type caravan parked in a clump of trees next to the 'Holy Well' stream from which they drew fresh water. Sam lived there in that caravan for most of his life.

On Friday, 24th May, 1935, in the 'Bolton Journal and Guardian', it was reported that a 'Disastrous Fire' had destroyed a large part of the Capital Works, which, since the closure of the Bleachworks in 1931 had been occupied by various small businesses. Some of these were destroyed and many were affected by the smoke and flames. It was reported that the fire started at 12.35 p.m. with a loud explosion, which was heard all over the surrounding district and is said to have shaken houses as far away as Church Road. It was described as 'Like Big Guns' or a 'Pit explosion'. The main building which is twenty-three feet long and thirty three feet wide was soon blazing from end to end. Within an hour the building was completely gutted, despite the fact that the fire brigade were soon at the scene. While firemen played their jets on the ruined building, members of the Hilldane Tennis Club which adjoins the premises continued to enjoy their game.

Some years later, during 'World War Two' my Dad, Harry Simpson was in the Home Guard, the headquarters of which were in Moss Bank House. Dad's Platoon met at the then disused 'Hilldane Tennis Courts' mentioned in the 1935 newspaper report. These were used as a firing range for small arms target practice, even though they only had two rifles between fifteen men. They took turns to fire at the target with blank rounds. Dad was in the Platoon for two years and never got beyond the rank of Private. He wasn't the best marksman in the Platoon, in fact, according to his friends, the

Commanding Officer called Dad over and said **'Simpson' if we let you loose with a rifle and live ammo we would have to evacuate Barrow Bridge,** and added sarcastically **"Don't have any aspirations to be a sniper".**

Mr. Cornelius Byrne employed by Mr. C. Howarth, Fruit and Potato dealer, was engaged in mending tubs at the time of the explosion. He said it lifted him off his feet. Next to the building in which he was working was a Wheelwrights Shop which was formerly the Fire Station at the Bleachworks. Also in an adjacent building was Jackson's Carting Contracting business and the premises of the Moss Bank Riding School. Mr. Tom Shipperbottom, the Riding Instructor, who summoned the Fire Brigade stated, that the explosion shook all the building and nearly threw him off his feet. There were three Hunters, two Hacks and two Ponies in the stables at the time. The cart horses were away. The building was soon showing signs of collapse. The floors fell in soon after the explosion and the fire spread to some other buildings surrounding the nearby disused bowling green. The amazing thing about the bleachworks fire was the speed at which it literally ate up the building. The smoke cloud passed over the Johnson Fold Estate and it was visible from the Horwich side of Chorley Old Road at Bottom o'th Moor.

From the old Fire station I turned left into Smithills Croft Road, down the hill and over the bridge passing over Dean Brook flowing to my right down the wooded valley towards Smithills Dean Road. As I walked down the hill I noticed, set in the angle of the road surface and the stone wall were a number of stones, set at a regular distance down the incline. These had been placed there for a purpose. This road was used frequently by the Bleachworks horses and carts carrying heavy loads of cloth. As the horses pulled the cart up or down the incline and the carter thought his animals were having difficulty controlling the heavy load, he would manoeuvre the cart towards the wall, slow the horses down and let the cart roll back to rest against the stone, thus giving the horses a rest before moving on. To my left is the old 'Drying House' on the front of which are those familiar initials J.H.A. and the date 1852. (John Horrocks Ainsworth). At this point I cross the bridge spanning Dean Brook below, carrying the matchstick on it's journey east behind the 'Prospect Works', to my right and on towards Smithills Dean Road. Directly after the bridge 'Croft Road', as it was called in the 19th century, veers sharply to the right following the direction of the brook.

I still haven't been able to approach Victoria Lake, which lies a short distance up stream. At this point I see to my left, a wide cobbled path or bridleway rising steeply from the road through woodland, which we knew, in the 1950's, as 'Bluebell Wood'. This path is heading in the direction of the lake. After only a few metres the silence is broken by the sound of running water. I headed through the trees and it soon became obvious that the sound I am hearing is that of the brook flowing through the valley from Victoria Lake, now clearly visible to my left. At last I had found the elusive Victoria Lake.

I returned to the cobbled path and followed it up the hill. After only a few minutes I emerged onto Smithills Dean Road, directly opposite the entrance to Smithills Hall. It soon became obvious to me that the cobbled path was the direct route for the Ainsworths to walk or ride from the Hall to the Bleachworks within minutes and was purposely cobbled to prevent the ladies of the family getting their long skirts muddied along the way. I returned along the path to Croft Road.

As I pass Beech Cottage to my left, I am reminded of the time I spent talking at length with my friend David, who spent all his early years growing up around Halliwell and Smithills. This is David's story:-

'Being brought up at the top end of Halliwell Road in the 1940's and 1950's, my friends and I spent many hours playing around the 'old bleachworks site which had closed some years before and now housed a number of small businesses. From here, we naturally migrated north, whenever we went out playing, up to the 'top forest', an area of woodland between Smithills Dean Road and Forest Road. Dean Brook flows from Victoria Lake, through the forest, behind the Bleachworks and on under Smithills Dean Road. From the 'Top Forest' we walked on to 'Bluebell Wood', Smithills Dean, Moss Bank, Barrow Bridge and the moors beyond.

If we were going to Smithills or Barrow Bridge we quite often went via the 'Top Forest', down to the river and over the bridge which brought us out through Croft Laundry and onto Smithills Croft Road. We would then spend some time looking through the windows into the laundry where we could see the ladies on the large rotating machines pressing what looked like large bed sheets.   There was always a lot of banter between these ladies and us. Facing the laundry on the other side of the road was a stone wall about 8ft in height, on the other side of which was what seemed like a swamp, but it was only narrow, always had water in it and there were a lot of rusty iron pipes around.   I now know they were part of the Ainsworth's water supply for their Bleachworks, but at that time for me, they were just old rusty iron pipes. Quite a number of years later the laundry burned down and I remember standing on the top of that wall watching all the fire engines in action'.

Carrying on up Smithills Croft Road towards Beech Cottage were more stone buildings on the left, but we didn't know what was in them because there were no windows for us to see through. About 100 yards or so before the left turn in the road up to the 'Big Chimney' there was a break in the buildings and in the middle of the area was a square raised platform which I remember being told had been for loading carts and lorries. Along the back was a stone wall with an old rusty iron gate in it, beyond which was the river and then there was a single storey stone building. The right hand side of the area again had a higher building, I think two storeys, which extended along the rest of Smithills Croft Road and round the corner. This building did have windows in, although a lot were broken and we could see inside many sacks piled up high. They were full of brown pellets which were soft in texture but had a rather unpleasant smell. I was told they were called 'Locusts', I don't know if that is the right spelling, and were for animal feed. I suppose it could have been the Carob Bean which is also known as the Locust Bean, one use of which is for animal food.

From Beech Cottage we would often walk up the narrow cobbled path and at the top we went through a gate and went straight up through the fields at the side of Limefield Reservoir. We then reached the rough path which ran from Smithills Dean Road through to Barrow Bridge passing Sheephouse Farm. We then turned left and followed the path which came out facing the Barrow Bridge Boating Lake entrance.

The Boating Lake had a special fascination for all of us and if we could afford it h we would hire a boat. There were four brothers and their sister who ran the farm, the brothers generally, but not always, did the manual work and their sister looked after them and did the cooking, but she could also turn her hand to any of the farm tasks if it was necessary. I occasionally helped out on the farm and once when we had been haymaking I was invited to join the farmers for dinner. We all sat around the table and enjoyed a lovely hearty meal. As soon as the meal was over all the men put their arms folded on the table, rested their heads on their arms and went to sleep. I didn't know what to do so I did the same. After about ten minutes or so they all woke up and got up to continue with their work, so I followed suit'.

Beech Cottage was originally four cottages built for employees of the Bleachworks, probably from stone from an adjoining quarry known as 'Beech Clough' owned by the Ainsworths. It is recorded that on two separate occasions in 1835 huge falls of earth and rock occurred. Each fall contained between three and four thousand tons of material. The noise of the falls could be heard throughout Halliwell. A large quantity of quarrying equipment was destroyed but no lives were lost.

At the rear of Beech Cottage, as early as 1845, a 'Tram Road' extended eastwards, crossing Smithills Dean Road to the coalmines of Smithills and 'High Lawn' on Smithills Moor.

The description 'Tram Road' was used to describe a rail track, either temporary or permanent, constructed in or around a mine or quarry (a delph) which was not part of the national railway system. The route of this track, based on the 1845 ordnance survey map suggests that it's purpose was to transport coal from local collieries to the Bleachworks. The track could also be used to transport stone from 'Beech Clough' to the site of the nearby 'Limefield' reservoir during its construction.

As we leave 'Beech Cottage' heading down Croft Road the 'Prospect Works' and the 'Dean Brook Valley' are to my right. Above the valley is 'Forest Road' a vivid description of which by T. Greenlees was published in the Bolton Chronicle on May 5th, 1909. He writes :-

A SPRING RAMBLE

By T. Greenlees

Bolton Chronicle May 5th, 1909

'I always hold that Bolton is not devoid of many a pleasant walk or even beauty spots and thanks to the electric cars we may be landed at the very door of these places of which there is none more popular than Barrow Bridge and SixtyThree Steps. The royal road to this place is no doubt Forest Road, which is at the end of the tram terminus of Halliwell. This road has not been formed many years, but its uses and advantage to the general public seems to have been inestimable and there is no doubt that many thanks have been silently voiced to the landowner for this gift.

The road is not only an ideal one, but the view that it commands on the north side of Bolton is indeed fine, especially at this time of year when the trees are bursting into leaf, and you can see in the distance all the varied colours of the trees in their Spring attire. After admiring the view in the distance from Forest Road, there are many objects close at hand that are worthy of our attention from a nature study standpoint. There are without doubt, a fine and varied collection of young trees mingled here and there, with some of the old trees that grew on the hillside before the road was made. There are at least sixteen different kinds, so that if one cares to know something of our own local trees, Forest Road is very difficult to beat if the length of road is taken into account. You find the oak, elm, sycamore, horse-chestnut, black poplar, beech, cracked willow, lime, mountain ash, elder, hawthorn and you will also find the two kinds of goat willow, the male tree and the female tree which is commonly known as the palm, and the wonderfully varied tints of the sycamore which all must admire. You also may notice the large buds of the horse chestnut, which seem to be covered over with varnish, for the obvious reason that the tree uses this as a means of protecting its young leaves from frost and cold. There are many other points of interest even on this road, but we must move on'.

'After we leave the road we pass the stile and go towards the croft, and in the meadow on the right hand side you may see a fine clump of 'celandine'. Instead of passing the chimney on the right, I think it is much pleasanter to turn to the left and go round by Moss Lane. We can see the large house in the distance which is known as 'Moss Bank'. This is said to derive it's name from the land around here being known as 'The Mosses'. As we pass along the lane towards the gate-house we must notice the fine old horse chestnut trees that are planted in the different parts of the meadow. As we pass the lines of the trees of lime, beech and sycamore, we come to the bridge and you may see in the water the large leaves of the water-lily. You can see clearly the wonderful manner in which the young leaves are curled up and also you may give a thought to the wonderful structure of the leaves of this plant which could not be explained in the article alone'.

The original 'Prospect' works was extended to include the 'Albion' works and during the early eighteen hundreds John

Horrocks Ainsworth was constantly adding to and making the Bleachworks more efficient and ultimately more profitable. The works grew to such an extent that by the mid 1800's it covered virtually the whole of Croft Road and along this length of Dean Brook flowing behind it. Approximately half way along it's length was a large loading bay, where heavy horses and carts were constantly loading and unloading cloth, making the road a hive of activity.

As we walk on towards Smithills Dean Road, passing the high wall to our left, above which are the lodges holding reserve water for the works, again on our left, we come to a detached building, this was the Smithills Estate office. A little further we pass a row of cottages, one of which is the Police Station and in the early 1900's, this was the home of the local Police Constable P.C. Hilton, 'a popular local bobby'.

We soon arrive at the junction with Smithills Dean Road. On this corner, to our left, is the distinctive chapel like property named 'Beggars Acre', so named, it is said, that in the 17th century, the Lord of the Manor (Smithills Hall) allotted this piece of land to be used by his tenants to grow vegetables to feed the local beggars. At this junction we turn right down the hill towards Halliwell Road, with the bleachworks to our right and the entrance to the 'Kier House', with the kiers sprouting great jets of boiling water onto the cloth. This and the nearby engine house, containing the great steam engine with it's huge flywheel were the noisiest and certainly the hottest places in the whole of the 'Prospect'. All the men working here wore clothing typical of the period, flannel shirt, flat cap, clogs and makeshift waterproof leggings. Most of these men lived only a short distance away in Halliwell and every 'Dinner time', around twelve noon, a group of school children, boys and girls, gathered outside the entrance to the Works holding large red handkerchiefs, knotted at the top, inside which, was a basin containing hot food with a saucer on top to keep the food inside the basin warm. Everyday these children were allowed out of school, with the Head's permission, ten minutes early, to take their 'Dad's dinner' to the 'Croft' and at twelve o'clock the workmen came out of the Works to collect their 'Dinners' and returned to their machines to eat the food - No Canteens in those days. The children then ran back to school. Dad had got his dinner.

We have now reached the point where Dean Brook flows under Smithills Dean Road and the matchstick has travelled approximately three miles on it's journey. This was the location of Smithills Mill.

Bert Jones, a family friend and a founder member of the Halliwell Local History Society wrote an article which appeared in the Societies publication 'The Little Piecer' In it he writes:-

'Recently, I was loaned a map showing Halliwell Bleachworks as it was in 1823. The Works at that time were not fully developed. That came later in the 19th century. Steam engines had been installed to drive the machinery, but one waterwheel remained. This drove the Smithills Mill which is described as a 'Corn Mill and Kiln'. In the first storey is the kiln, second storey is the drying kiln, third storey is a room for grain. In the Corn

Mill Room for sifting and weighing. Second storey is the Grinding Room with four pairs of stones therein and a storeroom for grain. An adjacent building contained the Water Wheel to drive the Mill.'

In 1823, the Mill was located beside the bridge that crosses Dean Brook at the bottom of Smithills Dean Road. Old maps and documents show that a Water Mill had existed hereabouts for hundreds of years in the area known as 'Milne Holme' in the loop of Dean Brook. Certainly it was there in 1620 when William Senior drew a map of the Smithills Estate for Sir Thomas Barton.

Mills usually belonged to the Lord of the Manor and his tenants were obliged to have their grain ground there. This practice was known as 'Millsoke'.

John Rawsthorne became the Miller in 1764. He spent considerable money on new buildings at the Mill and a water operated forge is mentioned when in 1800 he leased the Mill, land and water courses to Peter and Richard Ainsworth. There is no mention of the water forge, probably it had been absorbed into one of the Bleachworks workshops and become steam driven. From the map the Mill seems to have been quite a large building, about one hundred feet long, twenty-five feet wide and at least thirty feet high. It had four pairs of millstones which provided flour for most of the people of Halliwell.

In 1800, the population of Halliwell was about 3000. A tenfold increase from the number of 300 in the year 1700. Obviously, the Mill would have to increase in size over the years to meet the needs of a quickly growing population. It is highly unlikely that the Smithills estate ever grew sufficient corn for the needs of 300 people. To compensate for the shortfall, Smithills grew corn in Middle Hulton and Lostock.

It is not clear when Smithills Mill closed. It was shown on the ordinance map of 1846, but not on the 1892 map. It is assumed that it closed around 1870, during further development of the Bleachworks. The works expanded over the Mill site and Dean Brook passed beneath it. The passing of Smithills Mill severed one of Halliwells oldest links with the past'.

Just a short walk up the hill from the Mill site brings us to the junction of Halliwell Road. To the left is 'Temple Road'. I looked at the street sign and asked myself "**How does the word "Temple" suddenly appear as the name of a lane leading from the top of Halliwell Road, down the valley to the point where Dean Brook ends and becomes Astley Brook and is known locally as "Down't Temple" ?** The answer could lie in the diaries of John Horrocks Ainsworth.

In April, 1827, his entry reads:-

'Went to the old Church'. A few weeks later on the 19th June, he wrote, 'Went to the Temple Church and heard a sermon from Mr. Irving of the Chester House'. This statement is significant as, to my knowledge, this is the first time the word temple has been associated with the area. Could it be that the old Temple Church gave it's name to Temple Road? that a member of the Ainsworth family was a member of the 'Knights Templers', was one suggestion. This could, of course be true, but now we know the truth (or is it?) from the man himself.

What of John Horrock's statement *'Went to the Old Church'*. It should be stressed that this statement was written in 1827 before any of the Churches in the Halliwell area had been built.

So, there was a Temple Church, when? On June 16th, 1833, John Horrocks writes :- *'Hannah and I crossed the river to the old Church'*.

We have already established that the 'Old Church' must be the 'Temple Church'. Which way would he and Hannah come from his home at 'Moss Bank'? He would in all probability cross the grounds in front of the house to the junction of Moss Lane and across the road to a lane which later became Forest Road. They followed this lane to what was known as the 'Ginnel' to where it emerges onto Smithills Dean Road, such as it was at the time. Probably just a dirt track with stepping stones where the bridge now is. Could it be where John and Hannah crossed the brook to where the old Church stood? That is on the north side of the brook.

An area that could have accommodated a small building. A Church that has been completely forgotten, but did it exist? This story is disputed by some local historians and the Church that John Horrocks is describing is in fact the ' Temple Church' he visited in London. Will we ever know?

As we walk down Temple Road, my first recollection of which was in the summer of 1953. My friend Dennis and I had in 1949 started together as eleven year olds at Bolton County Grammar School. We sat together in class and became close friends, in fact some years later he was 'Best Man' at my Wedding. Dennis and I loved to play football, but we both hated cricket. The school used the playing fields at 'Barlow Park' which adjoins the Smithills Estate and every Friday afternoon, we, along with other boys in our year, wearing grey trousers, school blazer and cap, caught the 'Number 24 Halliwell' bus from Bradshawgate, round the corner from the school to the terminus at the top of Halliwell Road by the 'Ainsworth Arms'. We were supervised by a sports master and about thirty lads followed him from the bus, down Temple Road, passing 'Temple Bleachworks', which was originally an independent concern, but became, in the late 1800's, part of the Ainsworths Bleachworks. We then went on passed 'Holmes Cottages', built to house Temple Bleachworks workers. I later learned that my great grandparents, Mary and Samuel lived most of their lives, in the 1800's at number 11 the last cottage in the row before the 'Jiggling Bridge' so called, it is said, by generations of Halliwell folk, because it 'Jiggled' (moved) when you crossed it. At this point, Dean Brook is joined by Raveden Brook flowing through the Smithills Estate from its source on Smithills Moor.

Figure 14 Jiggling Bridge

The two brooks now become one. Astley Brook heading south west, under Moss Bank Way. Constructed in 1938, bisecting Temple Road, which previously ran uninterrupted alongside the brook.

Once my classmates and I had crossed the 'jiggling bridge', we walked up the steep path, with Raveden Brook in the valley to our left and the track leading to Moss Lea on our right. Arriving at the playing fields a few minutes later, changed into our cricket whites and played a game for two hours that Dennis and I found boring. This was repeated every Friday afternoon during the summer. Eventually we decided to 'play wag' from cricket and on a particular Friday, as the group got off the bus outside the 'Ainsworth' and headed towards Temple Road, we ran hopefully, unnoticed in the opposite direction. We ran a short distance down Halliwell Road to the 'Stork' Pub and into Dennis's home in Elliot Street, where Dennis spent some time trying to teach me how to play his upright piano, but I was more interested in watching 'Bill and Ben the Flower Pot Men' and 'Muffin the Mule' on their black and white television set. Some weeks later, we foolishly tried to 'play wag' again but our little scheme was discovered by a member of staff. We were summoned before the Headmaster, Mr. Grundy and were both given detention, we never did take to cricket.

As we leave the 'Jiggling Bridge' we noticed a unique smell, which hovered over the area. This was the 'stink' rising from Mr. Howe's piggery across the road which tended to make walkers quicken their pace as they walked by the brook. After crossing Moss Bank Way we arrive at 'Hill Mill' lodge to our right, originally a reservoir supplying water to a water driven mill standing adjacent to it. 'Hill Mill' was one of the earliest cotton mills in Halliwell. A plan dated 1816 shows the 'Hill Mill' estate belonging to Mr. Richard Constantine, described as a cotton spinner. The mill was probably re-built some years later, as an 1860 drawing indicating that the mill was indeed water driven using water from the lodge and discharging it into the nearby 'Astley Brook'. It seems unlikely that the lodge was entirely natural, it is more likely man made from a small natural lodge and possibly stone from it's excavation was used to extend the Mill and build a number of adjoining workers cottages.

Around 1922, the 'Hill Mill' site was acquired by Henry Crossley Packings Ltd. A company that had gained a reputation as a manufacturer of high grade, 'Hand Plaited' packing for the engineering industry. Henry was the second son of a family of seven brothers from Oldham. At the age of ten Henry went to work half-time, starting one week at 6.00 a.m. until 1.00 p.m. and attending school in the afternoon. The following week attending school in the morning and working from 1.00 p.m. until 5.30 p.m. A local businessman recognized that even as a ten year's old Henry was exceptionally bright with great potential and immediately employed him as a 'Plaited Packing' maker. Henry quickly grasped the essence of the 'Packing' industry and by the time he was nineteen years old he was already the foreman of Ritchie Leatham of Oldham. He continued his studies and in 1904 in his late twenties, he moved with his young family to London as Manager of a section of 'The British Ropes' Combine. In 1911 he became Packing Manager of Turner Brothers, which later became the multi-national 'Turner Newall'. Henry was a man of many talents and qualified at the famous Battersea Polytechnic in London.

In 1917 he started his own business manufacturing Plaited Asbestos and Graphite Packing for the engineering industry and was joined by his son Arthur, who served his apprenticeship in the laboratories of 'Turners' and father and son, with the help of Henry's wife Emma and their daughter 'Nellie' worked together tirelessly to develop the business. Arthur proved to be as talented and industrious as his father and even though he had trained as an industrial chemist, he became the engineer of the business and personally built a number of machines designed to increase the product range. All design, development and machine building was done within the family.

During the 1930's, the business prospered, the premises were extended a number of times and the workforce, mainly Halliwell people steadily grew. Every morning they walked from their homes in Halliwell to Cobden Street and down the steep cobbled path (which still exists to-day). This was originally built for the workers of 'Hill Mill'.

Late in 1937, when World War Two was a strong possibility, the Company was asked if they could develop and produce Asbestos Gas Chamber Pads for heavy guns used by the Army and Navy. The project was totally successful and Arthur Crossley appeared before the Royal Commission for 'Awards to Inventors'.

During the Second World War when most of the employees were women, Crossleys had been working twenty four hours a day, seven days a week and had been since 1938. When the war finished a good deal of re-building was necessary and the Company continued to thrive. Crossley's was indeed a true family business.

I decided on leaving the factory not to follow the brook but to climb the steep cobbled path as generations of workers had done before me. This took me along Cobden Street and on to 'Hill Top', a hamlet of approximately ten original stone cottages.

This is one of the oldest settlements in Halliwell with a fascinating history. Standing on a prominent outcrop overlooking the Dean Brook valley, the Smithills Estate and up to the distant Smithills Moor. 'Hill Top' was, in the 18th century a group of farm buildings forming what is called a 'Fold' (or 'Fowt') in the local dialect. A 'Fold' comprised a main farm building surrounded by other buildings such as barns, stables and the cottages of the farm workers who, along with their children, were also employed as handloom weavers.

Figure 15 Hill Top

As I enter 'Hill Top' I pass to my left 'Tootalls Park', known locally as 'Toot's Field', originally a farmer's field which became a public playing field in the 1930's. One of the oldest cottages was for many years the home of the Tootall family, the last of which was Tommy Tootall, whose father was the Carpenter to

Smithills Hall. He was a gifted wood carver who worked on many replacement carvings for the wall panels of Smithills Hall. The original farm and field were known as 'Toots' which most people assumed was a dialect interpretation of the name Tootall. However, most local historians including Derek Billington and Dr. Hanson took the view that the local families of that name derives from the early English word 'Toot' meaning 'Look' and 'Hill' from which a 'Lookout' could be made. In Lancashire dialect the word 'Toot' has survived to-day. I personally recall my elderly neighbours saying **"Ah see'd 'er tootin' behind t' curtains"** or **"What yer tootin at "**?

It is said that this hamlet originated in the 16th century when the lands around 'Hill Top' belonged to the 'Knight's Hospitallers', an Order of Monks who tended the 'Holy Well' that gave Halliwell it's name. On this land they built a Hospice (a place of rest and recuperation) for tending sick and weary pilgrims who were likely to have been fellow monks, travelling from Abbeys in Cheshire, calling at the 'Holy Well' on their way to Whalley Abbey.

Around 1540, Henry VIII, ordered his right hand man, Thomas Cromwell to destroy the monasteries. His minions carried out his order by attacking 'Hill Top' and destroying the Hospice, leaving just a pile of ancient red sandstone. Eighteenth century builders used those stones to build the older cottages we see on Hill Top to-day. Even in the 1930's, 'Dr. Hanson' who lived at 'Hill Bank House' adjoining Hill Top found sandstone blocks in his garden marked with religious symbols. These, together with local names like 'Cloister Street' and 'Holy Harbour' could substantiate this religious connection to Hill Top.

It is also said that the hospitallers had been forewarned of the possible attack on the hospice from the north and posted a lookout or 'Toot' at the highest point on the hill to warn of any invaders.

Adjacent to the cottages was a stone quarry owned in the 17th century by John Mangnall. Later the quarry passed into the hands of Thomas Heston, a Halliwell man who supplied the stone to John Horrocks Ainsworth for the construction of a number of local buildings including the 'Jubilee School' on Church Road.

As I leave 'Hill Top', I am faced with a most imposing building towering over the surrounding rows of 'Two Up, Two Down' terraces. This is the 'Falcon Mill' built in 1907 on the site formerly occupied by Brookfield Mill which was destroyed by fire in 1905. The Falcon Mill Ltd. was built under the supervision of architects George Temperley and Son, who described it on completion as *'a six storey building in red brick with bands of yellow brick and a decorative tower in one corner'*. It was described as one of the first Mills to have concrete filler joists, this enabled the floor area of the Mill to be greatly increased.

In the mid 1930's, the 'Falcon' was headlined in the Bolton Journal, when a Heron (very rare in Halliwell in the 1930's) appeared at the top of the tower. Some of the locals, not having seen one before thought it could be an 'Eagle or a Vulture'. Women feared it was a 'Stork' that might swoop down and snatch their babies from their prams. When it proved to be a harmless wading bird, crowds gathered on Halliwell Road, some with field glasses and telescopes to get a better view of the bird. Men and women going to and from work and children on the way to school, looked up to the roof of the tower, where the bird perched on the railings around the base of the flagpole. In those days the flag flew on 'Empire Day'. Sadly, the heron's visit lasted only a few days when someone shot the bird dead, whereupon the local steeplejack, Peter Hindley, had to climb the tower and dispose of the dead bird.

Figure 16 Falcon Mill

In the 1930's, a local historian tells the story of Jack, a young spinner who had been a 'Little Piecer' at the Falcon. He writes:-

*'I'm Jack I was born in Weymouth Street up Halliwell, just a two up two down and I was born the eldest of nine children. My dad was a spinner. He told me **"I saw Dowlings mill burn down, that's mill before't Falcon up Halliwell".** I can't remember seeing it, cos mi' dad said he had me in his arms as a child and we watched thow'd mill burn down, which was in 1905, so I was only six months old at the time of the fire. I started working at 'Falcon' in 1917 as half time 'Little Piecer', starting at six in the morning.*

I went on mi own ter't Education Office on Nelson Square near thow'd Infirmary. That's where you went for 'half time papers', which was a paper to say you were aged twelve and that your education had finished so you could start work. You had to have the paper to show your 'Gaffer' otherwise he wouldn't take you on.

*I wanted to be a 'Little Piecer', so I had to go to where there was a 'Spinner' who would take me on as his apprentice. Well't Falcon weren't nearest to where I lived, so I found out that a spinner from't Falcon lived in our street. I didn't know him, I just knocked on his door and said **'Can I be your 'Little Piecer' mister'?** It's a funny way of starting work, but that's how it was done in those days. When I was thirteen I left school and went working full time with him.*

Conditions weren't so bad at Falcon, in fact, it was only built in 1907 so it was only eight years old. It was a fairly modern mill. It was one of the first mills in Bowton driven by an electric motor. It used to break down pretty often, so you waited until it broke down then you could do your cleaning.

I was paid by the Spinner. When he drew his wage on a Friday, he was paid for what he had produced on his two Mules, then he would pay me, his 'Little Piecer' my money, about five bob and his Side Piecer his money, about nine bob and what was left he took home. That was the system. We were on a fixed rate, the Spinner wasn't.

Just after't War (First World War) I got Side Piecing and left Falcon when I was twenty and started at 'Holdens Mill' in Astley Bridge, but I enjoyed my time at Falcon'.

In an interview with a local reporter in the mid 1930's, Jim Morgan of Halliwell tells his dad's story:-

'My Dad worked on the construction of the 'Falcon' mill. His job was operating the hoist lifting building materials up to the top of the building. The hoist was worked by a steam engine, which meant him going to work early to get up steam for the day's work. He told of one or two incidents that happened during the building of the mill. One was when the scaffolding around the Engine House collapsed, leaving the bricklayers hanging onto the walls. One couldn't hold on, he fell to his death, but dad rescued another by climbing up a ladder and bringing him down over his shoulder'.

'Another incident happened when the top of the chimney was nearly complete. One of the bricklayers let slip one of the large, round finishing pieces as it was being fixed into place and it fell right down the middle of the chimney. Stood at the bottom, inside the chimney, was a labourer loading the hoist and hearing shouts from above, made a mad dash to get out. He was on the 'Run Plank' outside when the piece from above landed on the other end of the plank catapulting him ten feet in the air and unfortunately he broke his leg as he landed'.

'During the construction of the Falcon a night shift was in operation and after dark, in the winter, work carried on by the use of Lucy Janes which was rhyming slang for flames or flares fuelled by acetylene lamps. Dad worked on the 'Falcon' until it's completion in 1907.'

About that time my Uncle Wilf Brown was a spinner at the Falcon. As a young lad in the 1940's, I spent many happy hours with him on his 'Hen Pen' bordering the 'The Holy Harbour' sports ground where I would feed his hens and collect the eggs. Uncle Wilf gave me a small plot where I grew my first flowers. I never had an interest in growing veg. I'm sure that was the start of my lifelong interest in gardening. I vividly remember standing at the gate of his Pen on a Saturday afternoon watching the 'Big Lads' playing football on the Harbour.

Because of the conditions in the Mill spinners worked in their bare feet and unfortunately, while at work Uncle Wilf was hit by a runaway cain skip, part of which totally penetrated his left foot. After the accident he never worked again and was a cripple for the rest of his life.

Figure 17 Spinners

Bob Porter was born in Shepherd Cross Street, Bolton in 1903. He was the son of a mule spinner, his mother was a weaver. Textiles were in Bob's blood. In 1916 he started to work as a thirteen year's old half timer little piecer at Harwood's Mill in Darley Street, Brownlow Fold, under the supervision of, (as he was affectionately known) 'John Coffee', the spinner or minder. A name he acquired because he always drank coffee when tea was the accepted drink of the working man. Bob never knew his real name, but with 'John Coffee's' help and encouragement Bob went on to be a 'Side Piecer' and eventually a highly skilled 'Mule Spinner'. After forty years in textiles he wrote a poem which he dedicated to, in his own words, 'A special breed of man' who trod the 'Wheelgates' (the mule floor) always in bare feet eighteen to twenty miles in a ten hour working day. He writes :-

In the middle of the First World War I was barely thirteen years,
I followed the footsteps of mi Dad to share the family cares.
He had been a spinner all his working life,
An mi mother was a weighver afore she was a wife.

I started as 'little piecer' in a mill in Brownlow Fold,
The spinner who I worked for was getting rather old,
He had a pair o' Dobsons mules and he was proud of these,
And nursed them to perfection with skill and practised ease.

His nickname was 'John Coffee', a decent kindly chap,
He taught me how to piece and creel and sometimes gave a tap,
On those mules he spun fine yarns in the 80^s and 100^s range,
He spun those counts for months on end and never made a change.

I didn't seem to realize then in those grim wartime days,
That Lancashire was 'doing its bit' without much fuss or praise,
Wi' fifty million spindles we had to 'bear the brunt',
An't weighvers too turned out their cloth to help the lads at 'front'.

The firm of Richard Harwood was a strong trade union 'shop,'
Jack Battle was a spinner there and made them many a cop,
He was Bolton Spinners President and often had to deal,
With 'knobsticks' and other men who had no 'union feel'.

In our clogs we tramped to work to start at six o'clock,
The rooms were hot and humid so we never wore a sock,
We hurdled o'er those wheelgate slips in our bare and oily feet,
As't mules clanged to and fro from early morn till neet.

As't lads went up to fight the foe and face the Flander's mud,
promotion to 'side piecer' came too soon to do me good,
the spinner I now worked for was as different as chalk from cheese,
An' though I tried my damndest it was very hard to please.

My training had been far too short but I had to struggle on,
An as the weeks and months went by the sun ere seldom shone,
My spinner never taught me owt but I was keen to learn,
The action of those mules had gripped me so that the tide began to turn.

I went to 'Tech' three nights a week to learn the cotton trade,

and month by month I gleaned the 'nous' to help me make the grade,
No official of the firm encouraged me to my goal,
But a thirst for knowledge was the antidote to their restrictive role.

The war was o'er an't lads came back to take their rightful place,
An't rest of us were thankful we'd bin living by their grace,
As manhood came and I took stock to see what I had done,
I saw the same old spinner and wheelgate were I'd spun.

The prospects were depressing as one waits for 'dead men's shoes',
and thoughts of other pastures would often make me muse,
We decided we would make a break and change our doleful lot.

We'd heard of opportunities at Lostock Junction Mills,
So off we went to chance our luck, yes, even if it kills,
I handed in my notice after eight long, weary years,
But I was not surprised at all when no one shed their tears.

So at the end of this long and dreary lament,
It would be false to say that this was just my event,
Many Bolton lads suffered such harass,
But Bolton's motto sustained them 'Supera Moras'.

Bob Porter, April 1988

I have deviated from the brook, but I will re-join it shortly. From the Falcon I soon find myself on Halliwell Road, this part of which I know very well having spent a large part of my childhood at my Grandpa and Auntie Hilda's house on 'Rushey Fold Lane' which is just across the road, from where, on that September day in 1946 me and Grandpa started our walk to 'Brunt Edge'.

I am surrounded by stone buildings, which gives the impression that Halliwell Road is very old but, compared to other roads in the township this is quite the opposite. The road, then no more than a dirt track was laid down around 1805 and as it passed through the lower part of Halliwell it was called 'New Road'. At that time industry was starting to grow rapidly in Halliwell. Ainsworths Bleachworks was a large and important business to the community, employing many local people. Spinning Mills were also thriving, including Dean Mills at Barrow Bridge and the Temple Mill, owned by Pickering and Platt. All these concerns were powered by the fast flowing waters of Dean Brook, as did many other small businesses. The new road was necessary, because at that time, the only good, well surfaced road was the Bolton to Chorley turnpike (toll road) through Doffcocker. To get to this road (now Chorley Old Road) from lower Halliwell was via. what is now Bennetts Lane and Valletts Lane, down the valley, across the Ford at Doffcocker Brook to join the Chorley Road at what is now the Ivy Road junction. This was a long, steep and tiring journey for man and beast.

The Turnpike trustees, including Peter Ainsworth and John Pickering, stressed the need to the other trustees for a new road across this part of Halliwell. Consequently, in 1805 an Act of Parliament was passed for a new turnpike from Halliwell. This passed over Smithills Bridge and Dean Brook, along what is now Smithills Dean Road, past Smithills Hall to Bryan Hey, where it turned sharp left running past Colliers Row and Walker Fold to join the Bolton to Chorley turnpike at the 'Bob's Smithy Inn'.

With the rapidly growing industry in the Halliwell area, many more workers were needed and between 1801 and 1901, the population of Halliwell township rose from 1,385 persons to 23,953. The biggest rise was from 1801 to 1821, when in those twenty years the population doubled. Those were the years when Halliwell's industry grew rapidly and many 'Incomers' moved in from the surrounding countryside. More workers meant more houses to accommodate them, so the main employers, Ainsworths, Cross of Mortfield, Taylors and others began to build, thus creating more jobs.

Different sections of the 'New Road' were called by different names. Part was called 'Pilkington Street' after an old land owning family. Another was called 'Water Street'. This name, inscribed in stone is shown 'J.C. Water Street 1845' on the wall of the row of cottages adjacent to the 'Crofters Arms' pub.

By the time the earliest ordnance survey maps were made in the 1840's 'Halliwell New Road' had become a well built up area, with stone buildings on both sides of the road. Until 1877 the road was under the aegis of the turnpike trustees and their

'Toll House', built in 1824, still stands at the corner of Halliwell Road and Hargreaves Street.

I walk just a few yards further to, on my left, the tram Stop outside Mr. Fletcher's toffee shop where, in the mid 1940's my Auntie Hilda took me most Saturday mornings for 'two ounces' of my favourite 'Peanut Brittle' (peanuts in caramel) which was 'Off Ration' (not subject to wartime sweet rations).

As I reflected on those happy times, I was brought back to reality by the loud 'Clanging' of the Halliwell 'H' Tram as it slowed down for the tram stop. A few people got on and I heard the conductor pull the chord twice ringing the bell, telling the driver he was clear to move the tram on and shouting, which most tram conductors did **"We're off to Town"**. As the tram disappeared towards town, I walked to the end of the row of shops and arrived to my left at Peak Street, known locally as 'Peaks's named after an old farmhouse standing just down the street.

Figure 18 The Halliwell Tram

In 1935, Harry Simpson, who lived in nearby St. Thomas Street, would meet his girlfriend Elsie Peters, (She lived in Rushey Fold Lane) on this corner every morning, on their way to work, as weavers at Walter Mather's weaving sheds at the bottom of 'Wapping Street' and after two years of courtship they were married at St. Joseph's Church, Halliwell. Harry and Elsie were my Mam and Dad.

From Peaks's I walk along "Winter Street". On my left is the Salvation Army 'Citadel', where for many years the Salvation Army band was based. I remember the time when the 'Army' came round the local streets playing those rousing tunes and rattling their collection boxes for the homeless.

A member of the band in his memoirs, tells of a typical Christmas with the 'Army' band. He says :-

"The first Sunday in December we used to start, and we were out every night of the week. Then on Christmas Eve we would meet at 7.00 p.m. and go to Darcy Lever, then walk it back to Bolton. From here we would go to different houses and at almost every one we were offered a plate of potato pie, cakes and cups of tea". We were out all night until 8.00 a.m. the following morning when we would finish up at Eagley and we then walked and played all day. Oh, they were 'Happy Days' then on Christmas Day we had a social evening with Father Christmas".

It was time for me to move on and make my way back to the brook, passing rows of terraced houses, all with clean white net curtains, newly mopped and 'Donkey Stoned' doorsteps and painted window sills, reflecting the pride these Halliwell folk had in their homes and their streets. This area is dominated by mills, weaving sheds and factories and as I looked around me at this close knit community, I was greeted with a cheery **'Good morning'** by two passing strangers. I am reminded of a poem by a Bolton girl, Pat Wright. It reads :-

DOES THE TOWN WHERE I WAS BORN
BY PAT WRIGHT

Does the town where I was born
Still have it's New Year Fair?
Does the Town Hall clock still
stand so proud
With the lions in their lair?

I know the tramcars don't run now,
They vanished with the war, so,
Do buses run to Montserrat
and Doffcocker before?

They used to charge us 'tuppence' Goin 'all the way',
But 'tuppence' was a fortune then,
So we always walked halfway

.
Do Bolton folk still gossip
About their friends and foes?
And boast about their garden
And who's grown the biggest rose?

Do the curtains still get pulled aside
When a stranger passes by?
And do the steps get cleaned with stone
And then left there to dry?

In my little town the 'nets' were white
And the doorsteps sparkled too,
Wherever I have wandered since
Their like I never knew.

Is Smithills quiet by nine o'clock
When we would go to bed?
And is it quiet on Sunday,
as quiet as the dead?

Is my old house still standing there
with roses by the score
And old Jim's rustic fencing
And an ever open door?

Do the folks still rally round
If a neighbour is in need
With loving help and goodwill?
That was the Bolton breed,

Does the nightingale sing its song
Across the fields at night,
Do the children go to Barrow Bridge
to paddle in the brook?
And do they climb the famous steps
To get a better look at the
beauty that surrounds you?
It's an ever open book.

Nostalgia that remembering brings
Fills my heart, whether near or far,
Deep feelings distance cannot dim
And long years can never mar.

Such bitter sweet experiences
For all is done and said,
These memories are my childhood world,
Where I was born and bred.

As I make my way down the hill towards Astley Brook, I am now in the area known locally as 'Down't Mop', so named after the 'Weavers Arms the local pub, which stands at the bottom of Raglan Street above the brook. There are a number of local stories regarding the Pub's nickname 'The Mop' or 'Frozen Mop' and it's history.

Tradition has it that in the mid 1800's, the unnamed female Licensee, after mopping the front steps of the Pub, left her mop propped up to dry outside the front door and some mischievous local lads hid it. When the mop was eventually found it was frozen solid. The angry Publican hung it over the Pub sign as a warning to the culprits, where it hung for years. Some years later it was claimed, by the Licensee, Jim Tatlock that it was he who had, one cold morning finished his daily mopping and in a hurry left the mop standing outside the door. After some time it froze to the floor and remained there for many months. So the nickname 'The Mop' not only became associated with the 'Weavers' but with the whole district. Even the local kids called Astley Brook t'mop brook'. It is thought that the Pub was once part of a rather fine residence, standing in it's own grounds. A map dated 1850 shows a fine house, 'Beech Bank' standing on this spot which adds weight to the suggestion, the site would at that time be an attractive location on an elevated piece of land overlooking 'Sharples Vale', which I will visit shortly and must have been a pleasant haven of peace and quiet at the time. However, another account says the site was once a farm with spreading fields. Later, the extensive cotton mills of Messrs. William Tristram (known locally as 'Thrutchups' the origin of which I have not been able to confirm) put an end to it's agriculture.

Figure 19 The Mop or Weavers Arms

Stories passed down through the generations often prove to be the most accurate, two such stories from the Pub's past are still told in the 'Tap Room' to-day. It is said that at the turn of the last century and for many years, a picture said to be over two hundred years old hung over the bar. It depicts two curious looking characters whose names were Johnny Rosen and Charlie Beautshot. Both were beggars and the picture shows them confronting each other because Charlie said Johnny was poaching on his patch.

Figure 20 Dominoes in the Mop 1950

One of the 'Mops' most famous characters was 'Billy' the dog, belonging to Billy Unsworth, a local man. He became the 'Best Friend' of the regulars, and on the dog's passing, it was said **"He created a void that was difficult to fill"**. The dog's death caused so much distress among the locals, it was decided to give him a funeral. Billy Unsworth, carrying the dog in a wooden box led the 'Cortage', followed by five of the district's 'Best Folk', walked in procession to a garden, where the dog was buried and a memorial bearing the words 'Billy o't Mop' was erected.

Leaving 'The Mop' behind me, I walked down the cobbled road to Sharples Vale, once a thriving community which straddled the brook and built in the mid 1800's around the old mill, which was occupied at the time by Messrs. Greenhalgh and Murton, later to become Greenhalgh and Shaw's. However all that remains is a small group of 'well kept' properties facing the brook, which once housed the mills Managers and a three storey building, once part of Murtons's, now a small Confectionary Company manufacturing children's 'Penny Tray' sweets including my favourite, as a young lad in the 1940's and 50's 'Kali and Spanish'. Most kids in the area loved a 'Pennarth of Kali and Spanish'. We would go with our penny to 'Little Jack's' Toffee Shop on the corner of Carlisle Street and Mort Street facing Brownlow Fold School and Jack would give us a packet of Lemon Sherbut ('Kali') and a small liquorice stick. We would then walk home licking the stick and dipping it in the 'Kali'. Delicious! I can still taste it now.

The passing of the Old Mill in Sharples Vale removed the last vestige of the cotton trade from this area, where it had thrived since the 1780's.

Figure 21 Astley Brook

I cross the bridge and head up the hill to 'Skrike Fold', known locally as 'Skrike Fowt'. A quaint row of ten cottages, passing to my right the lodges that once supplied water to the local bleachworks, which stood here for many years, until demolition in the late 1800's. It is said that tradition is sometimes more accurate than what eventually becomes history.

Occasionally two versions of an event can be contradictory so we must make a choice, but whatever course is taken it is easy to see how accounts of bygone local events can be passed from father to son and so through the generations, whilst preserving the original eye witness account. For instance, a Bolton man could have said ***"There used to be a pond where so and so's is now".*** My grandfather told me and it is almost certain that there was such a pond and probably the old man caught 'Tiddlers' there in his boyhood.

The traditional story of 'Skrike Fold' is a sad one, but at the same time there is some humour in the tale. The details of which are :- In 1793, Alexander (Alec) Ward, who lived in one of the cottages, for some reason accidentally or otherwise, cut his own throat and stumbled from his cottage with a blood soaked shirt, crying **"Bury me wee'r I fall"**. He subsequently collapsed and died through blood loss in a nearby field and his last appeal was carried out. It is said he was buried where he fell. From then on the district became known as 'Skrike Fowt' because of Ward's 'Skrike' or cry. The word 'Skrike' was commonly used even at the time of my own childhood. The term 'she's skriking 'er eyes out' was common place. The story could have been forgotten but many years later, a workman digging clay in a 'Skrike Fold' field unearthed a coffin which bore the inscription 'A.W.46 1793'. A number of the older locals remembered that A.W. were the initials of Alec Ward and that he was forty six at the time of his death. Probably they had heard their parents talk of the tragedy. The remains were later interred in the grounds of Bolton Workhouse.

That was not the end of the story, in a column in the 'Bolton Journal and Guardian' on September 29th 1905, the writer asks *'Could the term Skrike Fold, be an interpretation of 'Eskrick Fold'*? This could be true. 'Eskrick House' from which 'Eskrick Street' later took it's name, was not far away and the man who owned it, Henry Eskrick was quite well known in the area, although not quite as well known as his son George. He died in 1806 and was a good friend of the Preacher John Wesley. It is related that George, while pacing out and measuring the land area for the building of the old 'Ridgeway Gates Chapel' in 1776 surreptitiously moved the marker pegs slightly and when asked why, he is reputed to have said **"To give another foot to God"**, so there are two explanations to account for the name 'Skrike Fowt'. Which is the true one? We'll probably never know.

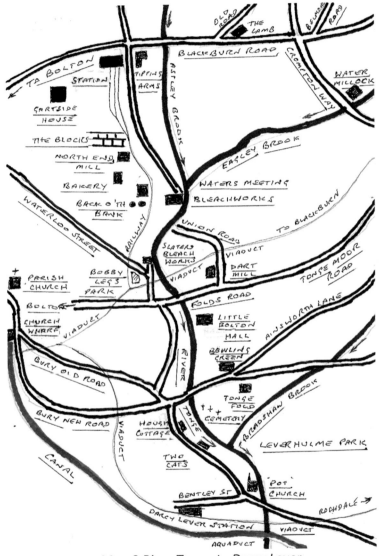

Map 3 River Tonge to Darcy Lever

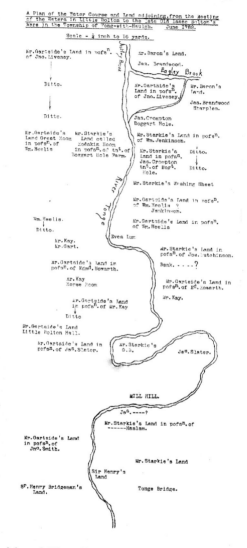

Map 4 River Tonge Landowners 1782

The matchstick is now fast approaching 'Astley Bridge' where the brook flows under the Bolton to Blackburn Road. I stood on the bridge carrying Blackburn Road, originally the Little Bolton to Blackburn turnpike or toll road, built around 1820. Just along the road, to my left is the 'Lamb Inn' built in 1823 at the junction of 'Old Road' which, before the construction of the turnpike was no more than a cart track connecting Little Bolton to Blackburn. Just around the corner from the Inn was a small yard, named by the locals as 'Tantrum Barracks' so called because, in the 1800's customers from the 'Lamb' had drunken fights there to settle their arguments. Sometimes wagers were placed on the outcome of the fights.

As I look closely at the bridge parapet I can just make out the outline of a date stone but it has been obliterated by a skimming of cement, probably during the Second World War. Even though I'm standing on the bridge that gave Astley Bridge it's name, this once peaceful rural valley before me is part of the 'Little Bolton' township. As I look down the valley into the distance I am faced with what I can only describe as 'Bolton's Engine Room', now providing work for over one thousand 'Boltonians'.

My senses are stimulated, sight by what I see before me, sound, I hear the sound of hundreds of workers clogs, tramp, tramp, tramping on the cobbles, making their way down the valley to start their shift in the factories and mills. Smell, a mixture of odours emanating from the valley including smoke from the numerous chimneys and the railway, steam from the bleachworks and power station. A hint of freshly baked bread from Warburtons Bakery in the distance and just to add to the atmosphere, the clinging stench of 'Piggy' Rice's piggery just behind me in Eckersley Road. Some sixty feet below where I stand, Astley Brook, carrying the matchstick flows from 'Heywoods Hollow', through a steep ravine, over a man-made weir and east towards 'Waters Meeting' where the brook is joined from the left by Eagley Brook to become the river Tonge.

Running parallel with Astley Brook is 'Tippings' Road, named after Thomas Tipping who became Lord of the Manor of Little Bolton in 1817. The first building on my left standing at the Blackburn Road junction is the 'Tippings Arms'. Adjoining the Pub on Tippings Road is a Smithy once owned by Henry, the local Blacksmith who in the late 1800's had a reputation of being a 'Ladies Man'. It is said that every day after shoeing the local horses, he left the Smithy wearing his best shirt and a top hat and headed next door to the 'Tippings Arms' where he would meet a different woman every night of the week and after plying her with drink took her back to his room above the Smithy for a night of pleasure. This nightly ritual soon became obvious to the Pub's 'Regulars', who when Henry and his lady left the Pub to go next door, picked up their pint climbed a flight of stairs onto a flat roof overlooking the Smithy window where they sat is comfort, pint in hand, enjoying the entertainment provided by Henry who was totally unaware of his 'Audience' for many months, or was he?

To the right of the bridge, facing Blackburn Road is the site of Astley Bridge Railway Station, now used as goods sidings and depot. This branch line or spur ran from the Tonge viaduct, part of the Bolton to Blackburn line at Folds Road. This line and the Station were opened in 1877. The passenger station was so little used that it closed two years later after running eight daily return trips to Bolton averaging five passengers per trip. However, the construction of Back o'th Bank Power Station, further down the line in 1914 brought a significant increase in goods traffic. Every day coal wagons were shunted into the sidings and 'Coalmen' from Astley Bridge and the surroundings areas shovelled coal into sacks and loaded their carts. One such Coalman, a local character named 'Forest Pike' set off every weekday morning at 6.00 a.m. with his two horses and cart from Belmont, arriving at the sidings one hour later. He loaded his cart for the return journey starting his deliveries in Belmont village about 9.00 am. People on Belmont Road often complained to him about the way he treated his horses on the long climb back to Belmont.

Overlooking the Station to my right is Gartside House, the imposing family home of the Gartside's who succeeded the Tippings in 1846 as Lords of the Manor. The house was accessed from Blackburn Road. Adjacent to this access and overlooking the valley is a large area of terraced houses known locally as 'The Blocks', so named because one of the streets 'Ulleswater Street' ran from Blackburn Road to a refuse tip overlooking the railway below. The street was used daily by Carters taking domestic and some industrial waste to the 'Tip'. However, because of the constant 'wear and tear' on the cobbled surface of the street, the cobbles were replaced with wooden blocks giving the street a smoother surface making it easier for the horses, hence the name 'The Blocks'. It is said that on a number of occasions the Carter lead the horse too close to the edge of the Tip and the heavy cart tipped over, rolling down the incline taking the horse with it into the valley below and many a horse had to be rescued from the base of the Tip.

Figure 22 Ulleswater Street "The Blocks"

Facing me, standing on the site previously occupied by what was known locally in the 19th century as 'Top o't Croft' is the 'Northend' No. 2 mill, built in 1903 and owned by the Northend Spinning Company, one of the four mills in this valley.

As we follow the brook towards 'Waters Meeting', to the right standing beside the Railway Line is 'Back o'th Bank' Power Station, discharging warm water into the brook. A real attraction for the kids from 'The Blocks' to play and 'paddle' in the warm water. A favourite game was to use their shoes as boats and follow them down the fast flowing brook, sometimes as far as 'Waters Meeting'. Many a kid's shoe was lost, probably floating alongside the matchstick to the sea and many a kid went home with only one shoe and a good 'Tellin Off' from Mam.

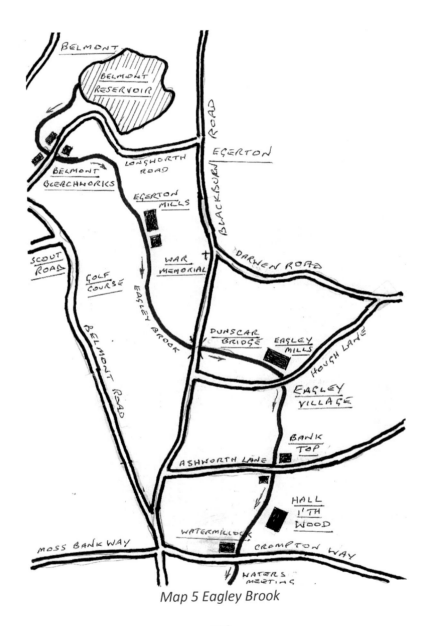

Map 5 Eagley Brook

We move on down Tippings Road. To the left is a footbridge crossing the brook to the site of a sewage works, brick works and allotments. Within minutes I arrive at 'Waters Meeting', or 'Meeting of the Waters'. It is at this point that Astley Brook is joined from the left by Eagley Brook to become the River Tonge. The source of Eagley Brook is the overflow from Belmont Reservoir and in turn the reservoir's source and gathering grounds is the surrounding moorland. As it leaves the reservoir it can be called either Belmont or Eagley Brook.

Around 1800 Bolton was expanding due to the industrial revolution and more water was needed to supply the thriving industries. The Reservoir was built in 1826 north of Belmont Village by Bolton Waterworks. From the Reservoir the stream flows down the east side of Belmont Village passing through Belmont Bleaching and Dying Works, originally built by Thomas Rycroft in 1880 as a Print Works. The brook goes onward through Shooterslee Wood passing the site where Longworth Mill stood until it's demolition in 1912. The brook then flows to the left of Egerton Village. It was here in 1826 that the Egerton Mills were built. By 1829 it had changed ownership several times. However, in 1830, the Ashworth Brothers, Henry and Edmund became the outright owners. The distinctive feature of the Mill was it's sixty two feet diameter water wheel attracting many visitors. The brook flows on towards Dunscar Bridge and Eagley Village passing Eagley Mills, built in 1796 by John Wakefield. Still in Eagley the brook then passes through open countryside passing the site of Taylor and Nicholson's Bleachworks built in 1900. The brook then turns south through a valley where new Eagley Mills stood. They were built in 1802 by John and Edward Ashworth.

Figure 23 Eagley Mills

It meanders towards the village of Bank Top and on through the Eagley valley, overlooked from the left by a building rich in history. This I the imposing tudor Hall I'th Wood, which was originally enveloped on three sides by an ancient oak forest most of which was to survive into the early 19th century, hence It's name Hall i'th Wood or 'Hall in the Wood'.

Built around 1483 as a 'half timbered' dwelling by Lawrence Brownlow who, according to the 'Brownlow Deeds' at 'Huntroyd' refer to a 'Burgeage Howse in Boulton', surrounded by 'a fine belt of timber'. Little is known of the Brownlow family but they were probably merchants connected to the weaving trade.

From the early 1500's the Hall was owned by a succession of wealthy merchants and yeoman farmers, including the 'Tonge's' the 'Norris's' and the 'Starkies'.

By the 1750's the Hall was leased to the Crompton family, whose son Samuel was born at Hall i'th Wood and was the inventor of the famous 'Spinning Mule' in 1779.

Figure 24 Hall i'th Wood

Around 1895 the Hall was in need of major refurbishment and was bought by the 'Bolton benefactor' William Hesketh Lever, later Lord Leverhulme, who totally restored the building to it's former glory and in 1900 it was presented to the town as a museum dedicated to Samuel Crompton.

The brook continues under Crompton Way to join Astley Brook at the site of Eden and Thwaites 'Waters Meeting Bleachworks'. Across the field from here is where two ancient landmarks once stood, both with unusual names. 'The Boggart Hole' and 'The Bottoms'. It is said that this field was used as a bleaching field by early outdoor bleachers. Some historians say that the Bleachworks was established in 1770, but the authority of this statement is not known. What is known is that in 1829 James Eden and Joseph Thwaites formed the Bleachworks under the title 'Eden and Thwaites'.

Joseph Thwaites continued to run the Bleachworks with James until 1856 when he died aged 54 years. Thwaites was succeeded by his sons, Thomas, Joseph and Edward. After his father's death Thomas bought out the interests of James Eden and William Harper and became sole owner of the business helped by his brothers. Edward Thwaites managed the Bleachworks while Joseph looked after the Manchester Markets of Eden and Thwaites and regularly travelled to Manchester returning in the evening on the Canal. The business thrived and in 1886 the capital employed was £120,000. It is said that in July 1856 there were 167 people under the age of 18 years employed at the Bleachworks. In 1870 Thomas Thwaites purchased, on behalf of Eden and Thwaites the property and estate of 'Hall House Farm' and his address in 1881 is given as Thomas Thwaites (Eden & Thwaites) Hall House Farm, Waters Meeting. On the land once belonging to Hall House Farm he decided to have a large house built for himself and it would be named 'Watermillock' after his ancestral home in the Lake District. Building commenced in 1880 but he never saw his magnificent home completed. He died in Southport on 21st October, 1882, aged just 49 years. The business continued until the early 1890's, when after a bitter family quarrell the brothers went into partnership with the Ainsworths of Halliwell. The works continued in various guises for a number of years and in 1939/40, it was then taken over by the Admiralty as a Royal Navy Victualling Depot and armed Admiralty Police were on patrol twenty four hours a day. It is said that the rum ration for the entire British Navy was stored there. No wonder security was tight.

Figure 25 Watermillock

During World War One, Watermillock along with 'Blair's' in Bromley Cross, became Red Cross Military Hospitals, treating many seriously wounded soldiers brought back from the conflict in Europe. After the War the house was used as a 'Retreat House' for the clergy of the Church of England and remained so until 1935.

At the time of the Spanish Civil War (1936-1939) Watermillock was used as a sanctuary for refugee children and was occupied by fifty refugee children from the war torn Basque province of Spain, most of them from the Bilbao area. A quote from the 'Bolton Journal and Guardian' on Friday, 11th June, 1937, reads: *'Fifty weary children fell asleep almost before they reached Watermillock on Wednesday night, the 9th June, 1937, after their long journey from Southampton. The children came from San Sebastion, Tilosa and Bilbao. Three or four are Roman Catholics, the rest being Protestant and various denominations and school lessons are to begin soon'.*

What of James Eden? He died in 1874 aged 78 years and in his Will he directed his personal Estate be sold in order to fund an Orphanage for the reception of infant children who had lost their parents and the trustees were instructed to spend a sum, not exceeding £10,000 on the building. It was built around 1877 and named 'Eden's Orphanage'

It's time to move on and I soon find myself standing on the bridge overlooking 'The Meeting of the Waters' with the River Tonge flowing into the distance. The railway line and sidings to my right, behind which is a cobbled path climbing steeply to the

'Waterloo' area of 'The Blocks'. Kids from the area were often seen carrying a bucket which they filled with coal collected from beside the railway line.

In 1904 a local character, well known in this area was George Thompson who was employed as a fire beater at Eden and Thwaites. Forty four year's old Thompson lived with his second wife Elizabeth and her two children. It is said he had a tendency to be jealous of Elizabeth, this was unfounded. She was a 'well respected' figure in the neighbourhood and earned her living making and selling herb beer which she brewed in the kitchen of her home. On Tuesday, 1st August, 1905, she retired to her bed at her usual time. Shortly before dawn on the following morning Thompson left the house and made his way to work. As he approached the Mill he was seen to remove his jacket and throw himself into the Mill Lodge. By the time help got to him he was floating face down in the water. His rescuers used grappling hooks to remove the now lifeless body from the water. In the meantime, after screams were heard coming from the house in Clifford Street, police entered the house to find two terrified children and the lifeless body of Elizabeth Thompson who had been beaten to death in front of her children. It was found at the subsequent Inquest that Elizabeth had been feloniously killed and that George Thompson had committed suicide, possibly as a result of insanity.

On the opposite side of the River Tonge from where I stand is Union Road and the cotton mills that dominate that area. The 'Dart' Mill built in 1906, 'Denvale Mills' built around 1880 and the oldest mill, 'Union Mills', built in 1876. These Mills hit the headlines in 1934 when the famous Rochdale born singer, Gracie Fields made a popular film 'Sing as We Go' and scenes were shot with the mill girls outside these Mills.

At the end of Clifford Street, overlooking the Tonge Valley is Warburton's Bakery. The smell from which hangs over the whole area.

In the early 1870s, Ellen Warburton loved to bake her own bread in the cast iron 'Range' at her home. Neighbours were soon attracted by the unforgettable aroma of Ellen's 'Home Baked' bread and were soon knocking on her door asking to taste it. Her reputation grew so much that in 1876, Ellen and her husband Thomas took over a shop on Blackburn Road which still stands and launched the Warburton brand. The business thrived and in 1915 a new bakery was opened in Hereford Street, close to the original shop, employing over one hundred people. It is now the largest bakery in the area.

Figure 26 A tram passing under Folds Road viaduct

The Tonge continues to flow south east, with the railway running parallel on the right approaching the Folds Road Viaduct, passing Slater's Bleachworks. This was originally known as 'Little Bolton' Bleachworks, owned and managed by James Slater who was the archetypal Victorian factory owner, much feared and disliked by his employees whom he ruled over with a rod of iron. It is said that 'Mr. Slater' had a pet goose that wandered around the works yard foraging for food scraps and one day was 'accidentally' run over and killed by a horse and cart. It was rumoured at the time that the killing of the goose had been a deliberate act of vengeance against Slater, who in January 1876, provoked a strike by his workforce by refusing to pay them for extra work to meet the deadline for delivery of an important order. The deadline for the order was fast approaching and in order to dispatch it on time, the Under Managers worked through the night to complete the work and those employees who had refused to comply were issued with dismissal notices. A week later others in the same association (forty one men and seventeen girls) who had also refused to work until their fellow members were re-instated were also issued with redundancy notices. As a result, workers gathered outside the main gate and formed a picket line. Because of his reputation Slater knew he had little chance of recruiting local workers to cross the picket line and resorted to advertising for replacement workers in Scottish and Irish newspapers offering free accommodation to those who would travel to Bolton to fill the vacancies. These out of town workers, who came mainly from Glasgow and Dublin were christened 'Knob Sticks' by the striking workers who were known as 'Turn-Outs'. There had been very little trouble on the picket lines, although the police were in daily attendance. However, trouble when it did come, was severe and merciless.

At 10.30 p.m. on Saturday, April 8th, 1876, three men left the Bleachworks and called into the 'Robin Hood' Pub for a drink. They were James McCurley, John Wright and forty year old father of three, James Thompson. The first two were 'Knobsticks' who were known as 'Beetlers'. The last man, Thompson was a local man who tended the boiler at the works. Although he had joined the workforce after the strike had begun, he wasn't a 'Knobstick', merely a new worker who had taken no part in the industrial action. Thompson was spotted drinking with 'Knobsticks' by a 'Turnout' who returned to the strikers and told them there were three 'Knobsticks' drinking in the Pub. All three returned to the bleachworks. Thompson was still officially on duty and still had to tend the boiler. The other two were returning to their cottages for a good night's sleep. As they walked towards the factory they passed under the railway arches of the recently constructed Astley Bridge railway line where they were attacked by a gang of men. The 'Turnouts' started by shouting abuse and were soon throwing stones. Wright soon ran off leaving the other two at the mercy of the strikers who began kicking and punching them. McCurley was kicked in the face and fell to the floor. He curled up to protect himself from the clog kicking. He barely escaped with his life.

Thompson had been due to fire the boiler at midnight before heading home. He was usually home by 12.30 a.m. 1.00 a.m. came and went. By this time his wife was very concerned for his safety knowing of the increasing tensions at the Works. She asked her neighbour, Sam Pilkington for help to find James and as they walked up Slater Lane towards the Works, passing under the railway arches they saw what they thought was a drunk lying on a piece of wasteland. They turned 'the drunk' over and to their horror realized this was the bloody battered body of James Thompson.

Three men were found guilty of his manslaughter and the Judge summed up by saying **"Will it ever be recognized that clogs are at least as deadly a weapon as knives and the revolver?."**

Around the end of the nineteenth century, conditions in the factories and mills of the North West were, to say the least, 'archaic'. The everyday life of a working man in the early 1900's was highlighted by this account of a Bolton factory worker. He recalls:-

'The largest part of textile machinery is made of cast iron, and that's dirty dust. You became like negroes on certain operations and at that time there were no washing facilities whatever for the workers and by subterfuge, the men introduced into the shop a bucket of water which used to be heated under the escape of a steam pipe. They had a tin with some soft soap in and another tin with some sand in it.

Towards twelve o' clock you used to sneak round the back of a locker and wash your hands with the same abrasive mixture of sand and soft soap. We were three of us doing this one day when the shop foreman appeared round the back of the locker, wearing his bowler hat as part of his uniform. He just looked at us and we were all dumbfounded, absolutely floored that he had caught us in the situation of washing our hands. He never said anything to anyone. He just pushed someone aside and kicked the bucket along the floor and walked back up the shop. I never felt so humiliated in my life and on the spot, I made up my mind, I'll see the day when men like you won't even dare to lift their foot to kick a man's bucket over. The workmen were conscious of how badly they were treated, but they were powerless because of the fear of losing their jobs.

Men were frightened for their jobs because of the large scale unemployment, particularly if they had families. They put up with the humiliation to hold on to their jobs. These were very often the people that ran industry, you were simply a clock number, you meant nothing to them at all. They treated us like Chinese dock labourers.

There were a lot of people actually starving. I think there's a lot of hunger now. I'd seen people collapse in the dole queue, through hunger. They'd been starving. One real cold winter there was plenty of snow, they used to queue up at Wellington Yard to get a spade to go snow shifting. I've seen men clear the snow in Crook Street and all that they had on their feet were a pair of running pumps, a jacket and a pair of pants. They shifted snow like that. It was abject poverty.

We had this placard going round the town and it were the time the police had started the cycle patrol and they made it as they had four shillings maintenance for their bike. A chap as was employed, he'd only two bob for his child. So we put on this placard 'Four bob for a Bobby's bike, two bob for a workers child'.

The Tonge continues to wind it's way through this industrial landscape of factories, bleachworks and mills. This whole area is dominated by the towering railway viaduct supporting the railway from Bolton to Blackburn. This section of the line was completed on the 12th June, 1848, comprising seventy three stone arches and at this point, on Folds Road in 1877 a spur was built carrying the railway to the Halliwell Sidings and Astley Bridge Station.

 Amidst all this industry and activity, overlooked by the Astley Bridge Viaduct is an oasis of greenery that is 'Darbyshire Park' in Slater Lane consisting of just two Bowling Greens where men who had worked hard in the mills and factories all week could relax with friends playing a game of bowls. The Park was named after Mr. J.C. Darbyshire, the first Mayor of Bolton in 1838, but to the locals it is known as 'Bobby Legs' Park after Robert Buckley, who in the early 1900's was the Park Keeper here and he is reputed to have had a 'Wooden Leg'.

An article appeared in the 'Bolton Journal and Guardian' on 18th January, 1829 headed 'How Halliwell, Astley Bridge branch helps Bolton industry.

'Perhaps the most important railway branch connecting industrial Bolton with the big world outside is that which joins the main line at Folds Road. Passing over stone built viaducts alongside Waterloo Street, this double line widens considerably in the neighbourhood of Halliwell and then, narrowing down again, winds it's way, snakelike to Astley Bridge where it terminates in a cul-de-sac opposite Blackburn Road. Inward trains are loaded with Egyptian cotton, iron, coal, flour and timber, as well as material for the bleaching of cotton fabrics. On the outward journey, wagons containing machinery and other finished articles collected from the districts of Halliwell and Astley Bridge, are despatched to the circulating depot near Manchester Road and forwarded on through trains to the Ports whence the goods in question are transhipped to different parts of the globe.

The first point of interest is the junction signal box above Mill Hill Street and the Folds Road arches which not only deals with main line traffic, but in a special way command the entrance to the Halliwell and Astley Bridge branch. The signalmen who work them in eight hour shifts always seem to be on the alert.

*A lecturer in railway economics at the Manchester University asked **"what would happen if a signalman slept at his post".** The assembled students pictured all sorts of eventualities, but the lecturer answered his own question **"nothing would happen if he fell asleep! The trouble might arise when he awoke. What would he do then? How would he act?"** and then it dawned upon the students that the regulations of the Railway Company actually covered a contingency of the kind, though no rule could ever be framed that would entirely obviate an impulsive mistake, should the human factor fail at a crucial moment'.*

Amongst all this activity, it is not only the signalmen who play a significant part in the smooth running of the sidings. Just as important are the 'shunting horses' and their handlers, who with specially made harnesses, manoeuvred heavy goods wagons from line to line, under constant threat of being crushed by runaway rolling stock.

In one of John Ruskin's works an interesting reference may be found concerning the manner in which shunting operations are conducted. **"Yonder poor horse, calm slave in daily chains at the railroad sidings, who drags the detached rear of the train to the front again and slips aside so deftly as the buffers meet and within eighteen inches of death every ten minutes, fulfils his changeless duty all day long. Content for eternal reward with his night's rest and his champed mouthful of hay. Anything more ernestly moral or beautiful, one cannot imagine. I never see the creature without a kind of worship".** If Ruskin had been living to-day he would have observed that the horse as a shunting unit is being superseded by a more potent force. That force is electricity. The power of to-day.

Standing by the side of the river, directly below the viaduct are a number of sheds and 'Pigeon Lofts'.
At the end of the 19th century pigeon racing was a popular hobby among the town's working men, who generally worked six days a week. Their only day off, where they could enjoy their hobby was Sunday, which meant they didn't attend church or chapel hence, 'pigeon fanciers' were frowned upon by the middle classes.

The arrival of the railways gave these men the opportunity to send their birds, by rail to destinations many miles away, where they were released by a rail- guard and flew back to their loft.

By the 1930's, pigeon racing became extremely popular, generating huge amounts in wagers. Most of the 'Fanciers' were real characters. One such character, who's loft stood below the viaduct was known as 'little Ray', who, as the nickname suggests was a man of 'short stature', no more than five feet tall, who it is said, every Friday night, visited all the Pubs in Folds Road area wearing his best clothes, including flat cap, waistcoat with 'fob watch' and polished clogs with shiny brass rivets. Ray had a friend, we'll call him Bill, who was an Engine Driver. The two had an 'Arrangement' where, when Bill's train was passing over the viaduct he would pick pieces of coal from the tender and as he passed over Ray's pigeon loft he would drop the coal down to Ray's plot for Ray to 'dispose of'. Unfortunately, one day Bill dropped a large 'lump' of coal, which fell through the roof of the loft killing two of Ray's prize pigeons.

At this point the Tonge flows under Turner Bridge, over which 'Folds Road' carries traffic from Bolton to Tonge Moor and beyond. In the mid 1800's, Folds Road was notorious as an area of petty crime and prostitution. However, one particular crime was by no means 'petty'. It is said that in 1842, Betty Eccles, a woman of ill repute who lived on Folds Road, callously killed her step-children by feeding them a pudding laced with poison. It was highly likely that Betty was insane, but nevertheless she was found guilty and hanged at Liverpool in 1843.

Most crime in the area was fuelled by drink, as was the case of Patrick McKenna and his wife Ann. She was murdered at their home in Kestor Street, Mill Hill, on Monday the 30th September, 1901, after a violent domestic argument, a common occurrence in the household, often caused by McKenna's addiction to drink. A Joiner by trade, but because of his excessive drinking he could only find casual labouring work. After spending most of that day drinking heavily in the local pub he arrived home to be confronted by his wife, who had resorted to pawning most of their possessions to 'make ends meet'. The argument escalated into violence and Ann was stabbed in the neck with a kitchen knife and within minutes had bled to death.

When McKenna realized what he had done he fled the house and hid in the house next door. Hearing the 'commotion' from the McKenna's, neighbours alerted the police who discovered McKenna cowering under the stairs of the adjoining house. After a struggle he was arrested and later charged with his wife's murder. After a trial he was convicted and was executed at Strangeways Prison on 3rd December, 1901. James Billington, the hangman died just ten days after executing 'Paddy McKenna'.

As the river emerges from Turner Bridge it flows past 'Little Bolton Hall' reputed to have been built in the 1300's. In the 1700's, this part of the Tonge valley would have been very picturesque with the Tudor Style Hall standing on the banks of the river, flowing on to 'Mill Hill', one of the oldest parts of Bolton. The area is now dominated by the Mill Hill Bleachworks, originally a water driven Corn Mill, which towards the end of the 18th Century became an extensive textile centre developed by Peel and Ainsworth, the principal partners being Sir Robert Peel and Thomas Ainsworth. To-day the Bleachworks is owned by Messrs Blair and Sumner. The Blair family were of Scots extraction and were, it is said, part of the Glencoe clan of McDonald who escaped from the terrible massacre of 1692. After the Jacobite rising of 1715, the first Stephen Blair escaped to Lancashire and settled in Manchester where he died in 1808. His son George who was a well respected employer who founded the Bleachworks, was on his death carried to his grave by his own workpeople. His descendant, another Stephen Blair is remembered for his generosity, including the funding and building of his Convalescent Hospital at Bromley Cross.

Figure 27 Little Bolton Hall

The matchstick is fast approaching the bridge carrying the main road from Bolton to Bury. High to the left, on the corner of Ainsworth Lane stands a most imposing building, the Bowling Green Inn, said to be over three hundred years old, this was also referred to as 'Ben Crook's' after a local character who once lived there. At one time the building was not only a pub but also a farm. The old farm buildings were known as 'The Studs', a name dating from the time when races were held on land opposite the old Inn.

Figure 28 The Bowling Green Inn

As the river emerges from Tonge Bridge, to the left is the huge area of Tonge Cemetery, a borough Cemetery since 1856 and the final resting place of generations of Boltonians. One 'resident', Thomas Maccarte was not a Bolton man, his background is a mystery. He may not even have been an Englishman. Maccarte was a thirty four year old 'Lion Tamer' who, in 1872, arrived in Bolton as part of 'Manders Travelling Manageri' a travelling Circus Company which moved from town to town throughout the north west. On Wednesday, January 3rd, 1872, at 10.30 p.m. on Bolton Town Hall Square, the Circus was giving a farewell performance before moving on to Bury. Maccarte, who's professional name was 'Maccarte the Lion Tamer' entered 'the cage' containing five lions. Occasionally these confrontations between man and beast could end in disaster. Maccarte was described by his 'Mentors' as over confident with dangerous animals and took his profession to the limit by taking sometimes unnecessary risks. Having already lost part of his arm to an asiatic lion.

This particular night the atmosphere in the 'cage' seemed unusually tense as Maccarte started his performance with one animal known as 'Tyrant', which earlier that day had bitten his hand, suddenly became aggressive and attacked Maccarte. The usual safety precautions were ineffective and the other four lions joined in the attack. Within minutes Maccarte was ripped apart before anyone could take action to stop the tragedy. The lions were eventually shot dead or driven away from the victim using 'hot irons'. Maccarte was fatally injured and died some hours later. Most of his body parts were recovered from the scene and he was buried here in Tonge Cemetery.

Overlooking the Cemetery is the Community of 'Tonge Fold' or 'Tum Fowt' as it was known colloquially. A hamlet of weavers cottages surrounding the local ' beer house', known locally as the 'Old Dug 'n' Kennel', once the hub of the community. The pub dates back over three hundred years and at one time boasted 'quaint rooms, scrubbed stone floors, roaring open fires and beer straight from the wood', drunk from pewter tankards. The highlight of the year in 'Tum Fowt' was 'Oak Apple' day, May 29th, when an oak effigy of King Charles the second was displayed in the tree outside the 'Kennel'. The event celebrated the escape of the Monarch from those who pursued him by hiding in an oak tree, but for 'Tum Fowters' it was an excuse for a good 'booze up'. As soon as the effigy was hung in the tree there would be a mad scramble of folk, as old records say *'hugging and kissing it'*. Perhaps this was due to the amount of free beer for everyone on the day.

Sometimes the eating and drinking went on for a week. Not surprising that this was the only place of entertainment in the area. Oak Apple Day was the highlight of the social calendar and included a Fair with Menagerie and Marionette Show. But the pub had other uses. As early as 1811, local people were holding Methodist meetings and by the mid 1800's they were held in the parlour of the 'Dug 'n' Kennel'. To-day, Bury Road is some distance away, but at one time the curved, cobbled main road from Bolton to Bury passed by the pub's front door and along the side of the building. The pub also had it's own supply of Well water, which perhaps accounts for it's reputation for having the best beer for miles. The Well is marked on a local map of 1723 when the next, nearest water supply was a spring at Breightmet. Artifacts have recently been discovered at the back of the pub including old clay pipes and metal tokens which a local employer used to issue to his workers instead of money. This way, they were forced to buy all their needs from his shop, which was the only place the tokens could be exchanged.

During the 'Great Flood' of 1866, it was reported that a number of coffins were seen floating from Tonge Cemetery as far downstream as the Irwell at Ringley bridge. As I walked along the path with the river to my right and the graves of so many 'loved ones' to my left, the silence was broken by the sound of digging. I looked round a particular ornate monument to my left and saw two heads complete with 'flat caps'. The rest of them was five feet down in a grave. They stopped work and looked up at me and decided it was near enough dinner time. As they climbed out of the grave we said our 'good mornings' and they joined me on a nearby bench, opened their 'butty bags', filled their 'brew cans' and over their 'dinner', introduced themselves as Dan and Bert. After passing the time of day the conversation gradually lead to their experiences working in the cemetery. Dan was the more philosophical and started by saying **"one of the first things we were taught was a gravedigger must never forget that the dead were once alive. They're people who deserve dignity and respect'.** He went on to say **'this is the world's oldest profession. I have dug graves for friends, relatives and complete strangers".** He recalled his early days in the job and told of how older gravediggers tried to forewarn them of the more unpleasant parts of the job, dropping hints and veiled warnings of the necessary tasks that they would have to do during the normal working day. By this time they had both finished their lunch and were soon pulling on a 'Woodbine'.

Dan was a man of some stature, well over six feet tall. He was the more 'outgoing' and from what he had already said, nothing seemed to phase him, but he told me of the day he thought he was going to die by being buried alive in a grave he was digging himself. He recalled **"It was about five year back, I was digging my first nine footer, I was at the bottom, the sides of the grave had been 'spragged' (strengthened) with timbers when, all at once, there was a hell of a crack and one side collapsed and I was engulfed in 'wet sand' which was pulling me down. I couldn't move and shouted for help. Bert heard my call, grabbed a plank and wedged it against the sides of the grave,** halting the flow of the wet sand. He stayed in the grave with me while I was up to my knees in sludge. He lit a fag and handed it to me and said casually 'we're having one of those days, are'nt we Dan', then we both started to shout for help. After about ten minutes, as we hoped, our friend Arnold or 'Big Arnie' as he was known appeared, peering down at us, up to our knees in sludge and 'tutting', the way he did. He undid his leather belt, and holding on to one end he threw the other end down for Bert to grab hold of. I hung on to him and 'Big Arnie' pulled us both out. The three of us have worked together ever since". Bert, Dan and Arnold were obviously good friends after their many experiences together. I left them to do their digging.

I am now heading in the direction of Darcy Lever, but I'm still in 'The Haulgh' district. Above me, to my right is 'Haulgh Cottage', built in 1836. A distinctive building owned by a popular local character, Tommy Hindle, a 'smallware' or general dealer. Anything you wanted, you name it, Tommy would get it, at a price.

I move on and again to my right is a gothic style gatehouse, known locally as 'Two C', showing two Cats, so called because on the front of the building is the Coat of Arms of the 'Earl of Bradford' the rampant lions. The building was constructed in 1854 and used as a park keepers lodge to the Bradford Park Estate, part of which was sold to Lord Lever who donated it to the people of Bolton in 1919 and opened by the Mayor of Bolton for their 'health and recreation'. This is Bolton's oldest park, named Leverhulme Park.

Figure 29 Two Cats

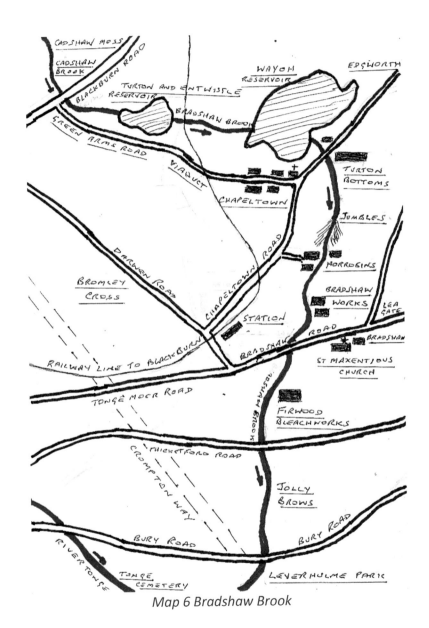

Map 6 Bradshaw Brook

I continued to follow the river passing a sign to my left pointing to the park and 'Oakenbottom', an area of oak trees where the Tonge is joined by 'Bradshaw Brook', flowing from it's source, some two miles north, high above Bolton as 'Cadshaw Brook' on 'Cadshaw Moss' and is joined by a number of other tributaries to form 'Bradshaw Brook' flowing south through the Yarnsdale Valley. 'Dale', meaning valley is common in Yorkshire place names, but rarely found in Lancashire. The brook then flows into the Turton and Entwistle Reservoirs, constructed in 1838 to supply adequate fresh, clean water to the area's growing industry in the Bradshaw valley. This valuable supply of water was the catalyst for the development of the Bradshaw and Harwood townships.

Figure 30 Old Pack Bridge at Turton Bottoms

The Romans built water driven corn mills along this valley which in medieval times was heavily wooded, suggested by the ancient English word 'Broadwood', from which the word 'Bradshaw' derives. The area remained primarily agricultural until the end of the 18th century. There is evidence of a water driven Corn Mill, 'Bradshaw Mill', which was in operation until the early 1800's.

Coal had been mined in this area from the early 17th Century and probably earlier. It is said that during the construction of the Roman road, 'Watling Street', which ran from Manchester to Ribchester, through 'Affetside', the road builders had a steady supply of coal from their excavations. During the 18th Century a wedged shape outcrop was discovered which stretched from Bradshaw to the Affetside slopes, this became known as 'Upper Mountain Mine'.

The word 'Affetside' is a combination of two ancient English words. 'Ofer' meaning a border or margin and 'Side' referring to the side or slope of a hill. This combination could be interpreted as a 'boundary on a hillside'.

From these early beginnings collieries at both Bradshaw and Harwood thrived throughout the 1800's. The workings of the Harwood colliery covered a wide area up to the Harwood boundary with Affetside. Both these mines were 'worked out' by the end of the century. However, some thirty years later, around 1930, James Yates and his family were living at a property known as 'Number Two Bungalow', Watling Street, Affetside. James had lost both his legs in the 1914 - 1918 War and had two artificial legs fitted. He had worked as a miner before the War at Tonge Colliery. The bungalow had no mains water supply, so James and his son decided to sink a Well on their land. James obtained explosives from a nearby quarry and blasted and dug down to a depth of approximately thirty feet, where they came upon old mine workings and had to go down a further ten feet to reach water. Some months later the Well was completed and a steady supply of water was maintained.

Father and son then turned their attention to the mine workings, which they later learned were the long abandoned tunnels of 'Windy Hill' Pit, which would give the family unlimited coal for domestic use. The coal seam was found to be nearly two feet thick. A hand operated 'bucket' system was devised to haul both water and coal from underground. James, minus his wooden legs (he found it easier to work without them) hewed the coal, while 'Jim Junior' hauled it along the tunnels and up to the surface. This process carried on well into the late 1930's, until James and his family left the bungalow which, just recently was demolished and the Well along with the entry to the pit was filled in. Only a barbed wire fence now marks all that remains of 'Windy Hill Pit'.

From the reservoirs, the brook flows under the viaduct carrying the railway line from Bolton to Blackburn, and on to the Wayoh reservoir, built in 1876 to meet the ever increasing demand for water to satisfy the thriving industries and growing population of the Bradshaw valley.

Figure 31 Viaduct over Bradshaw Brook

'Wayoh' is thought to originate from the old English word 'Weg', meaning 'Way' and 'Hoh' meaning 'Hill', the combination of the two words meaning 'a path over a hill'.

The reservoir takes it's name from nearby 'Wayoh Fold', once a small weaving and farming community which stood on a hill near 'Edgworth' and 'Broadhead Brooks', the two main feeder streams for the reservoir. Bradshaw Brook continues it's journey south through 'Turton Bottoms' and on to 'Jumbles', a variation of 'Dumbles', meaning a ravine or wooded valley through which flows a fast flowing stream. The brook gathers pace over the 'Jumbles Weir' and south to Horrobin Mills, comprising two groups of buildings, one on each side of the brook. Developed around 1780 as a small bleachworks by James Ainsworth, the younger brother of Peter Ainsworth (known as 'The Opulent Bleacher') of Halliwell. During the early 1800's, the works were owned by Thomas Appleton. The business thrived until September, 1870 when Appleton died at his nearby home, Horrobin House, leaving his son, William, a single man, to run the Mill. William had suffered ill-health for most of his adult life and in October, 1883 it was announced in the 'Bolton Standard' - *'Shocking suicide of Master Bleacher at Turton'. On Monday, a.m. about 10.30. the body of Mr. William Appleton, 45 years of age, proprietor of Horrobin Mill Bleachworks, Turton, was found hanging in a closet near the Mill, being suspended by a piece of calico. The body was later removed to Horrobin House.* The Appleton family continued to operate the Mill until 1903 when the business was put up for auction, but was not sold until 1905 when Robert Kenyon, a Timber Merchant, of Lancaster purchased Horrobins for approximately £40,000 and continued bleaching and dying until it was sold to the 'Bleachers Association' in 1937.

Robert Kenyon had been a well respected employer in the area and was very supportive of the district and many of the local people, including his own employees who regularly enjoyed a weekend walk through 'The Jumbles', passing Horrobin Mills.

Just half a mile downstream is 'Bradshaw Hall' and Works. The Bradshaw family of Bradshaw Hall had been Lords of the Manor since medieval times and probably earlier. The estate was based on agriculture and remained so until the end of the 18th Century. However, in March, 1816, a copy of the 'Manchester Mercury' reads:-

'Bradshaw Hall Bleachworks, with immediate possession to be sold by auction'.

'A capital mansion called Bradshaw Hall, also a most desirable Bleachworks'.

It was eventually sold to John and James Slater who operated the Works until 1834, when it was leased to Thomas Hardcastle, who, some years earlier had founded another successful business, 'Firwood Bleachworks', and lived at 'Firwood House', with his wife, Ann.

The 'Bradshaw Works' flourished under Hardcastle, who, in 1838, was instrumental in the construction of Entwistle Reservoir. One year later Thomas Hardcastle died at his home at Firwood and 'The Works' was taken over by his son James, who, in turn was succeeded by his son Thomas.

In the early 1800's, working conditions in the mills and factories, especially for women and young children were, to say the least, harsh and in some cases, very cruel. However, the 'Factories Act' of the mid 1800's, significantly improved the conditions of the working man and his family and in the 1870's,Thomas Hardcastle, as a responsible employer, with the welfare of his employees in mind, fully complied with the regulations, even bringing young boys and youths into the Bradshaw Works from Children's Homes and Institutions from Manchester and Liverpool. They were looked after by local cottagers whilst learning a trade at 'The Works'. This arrangement continued into the 1930's when the 'Works' was operated by Colonel H.M. Hardcastle, a military man who took over after the death of his father Thomas in 1902.

The early 1900's, were a period of steady expansion and with that success a number of employees steadily increased and by 1910 it became obvious to the 'Colonel' that a new power source for 'The Works' was necessary and the power of steam was introduced. This modernization meant that difficult decisions would have to be made. One such decision was to make 'The Works' three remaining draught horses 'Captain', 'Jack' and 'Lion' redundant.

The horses were described as being quiet and good workers'. These horses had given many years of loyal service to 'The Works' and were looked upon as old friends by the stable hands and carters with whom they had worked for years hauling their loads across Lancashire in all weathers, were to be replaced by steam driven motor lorries. The horses were taken by a local farmer, with the promise of a long and contented retirement and were regularly visited by their 'old workmates'.

In March, 1932, Bradshaw celebrated the visit of H.R.H. The Duke of York, later to become H.R.H. King George VI, to Bradshaw Hall and Works, during his industrial tour of Lancashire. No doubt influenced by Colonel Hardcastle being a Deputy Lieutenant of Lancashire.

The famous 'Bradshaw Flood' occurred in August, 1927, causing considerable damage to the community. A summer storm caused a build up of water from the Affetside hills which rushed down the 'Riding Gate brook' causing extensive flood damage not only to Bradshaw Hall and Works but a number of properties in the village itself. The local 'Smithy' was the first building to be struck by the torrent. A wall of water crashed through the back door and out at the front. Two Blacksmiths who were shoeing a horse at the time managed to dive out of the way, but the horse was carried so far and so fast by the force of the water, it wasn't found until four hours later, unharmed, grazing in a nearby field.

The properties mainly affected were the 'Smithy' and the cottage belonging to George Barnard and his wife. George's shed was swept away and was last seen floating past the Church heading down Bradshaw Brow. The Barnard's were unable to keep the water out of their home and when the flood subsided, a thick deposit of slime had to be removed from everything on the ground floor.

Figure 32 Bradshaw Smithy

The wall of water had surged through St. Maxentius Churchyard, damaging a number of gravestones and some graves were disturbed. However, the Church itself, built in 1872 on the site of the ancient 'Chapel of Ease' and the separate tower with it's equally ancient bell, dating from the 1500's, were left relatively undamaged. Although substantial damage was done to a number of surrounding properties.

My Grandpa Peters recalled having great difficulty, on the morning after the deluge, walking to his work at nearby 'Harwood Vale' Bleachworks passing, as he described them as 'The Church without a Steeple and the Steeple without a Church'

Figure 33 Bradshaw Church

It was reported, at the time that no one had been harmed by the flood and *'Bradshaw brook took all the water that came into it and no harm befell any cottage or anyone by it's side'.*

The brook continues under Bradshaw Brow Bridge soon passing Firwood Bleachworks, also owned by Hardcastle and on through, what is now a derelict area. Originally, in the mid to late 1700's, this was 'Ellis Fold', once a picturesque agricultural hamlet bordering the brook. To-day, however, all we see is all that remains of the long demolished 'Cadershaw Bleachworks' and it's lodges, now a favourite playground known by the local kids as 'T' Jolly Brows' and on under Bury Road to Leverhulme Park to join the 'River Tonge'.

I leave the park and walk down the hill towards Darcy Lever. To my right is a small community of terraced houses and cobbled streets, centred around 'Bentley Street'. At the end of which is 'Darcy Lever Station' standing on the main railway line from Bolton to Bury. As I stood by the Station I looked to my left towards the 'Lever Bridge' viaduct spanning the Tonge Valley with the river 100 ft. below thinking 'what a magnificent structure', when I heard a friendly 'Hy'a' beside me, it was Alan and his pals, a group of local lads. Alan told me that they had all grown up by the railway. We stood on the footbridge over the track just as a local train passed beneath us into the Station and for a few minutes I and the lads were enveloped in smoke and steam. Then my new friends and I descended the steps onto the platform. I was then introduced to their friend 'Ernie', the Porter, but were soon met with a 'wagging finger' by Mr. Brindley, the Station Master for distracting 'Ernie' from his job.

Alan and his 'mates' were avid 'train spotters' and had already taken the number of the engine standing by the platform. But the main attraction of the day, as far as the lads were concerned, was the 'nine o'clocker', the Blackpool to Rochdale Express which passed through Darcy Lever Station at nine o'clock every evening and was usually pulled by a 'Jubilee' class engine or, as the lads called it 'a Jub'. Alan described their excitement as, on winter nights they waited for the 'Nine o'clocker' racing across the viaduct and through the station with the steam, smoke and the glow from the firebox as it raced past.

Alan and his pals, Peter, John and Duncan, decided to show me 'their Darcy Lever', which is often referred to as 'Dolly Tub City' a title which stems from the village's industrial past, but the village has a heritage stretching back over several centuries. There was a time when the whole area was thriving with pubs and factories providing work for everyone. It was the area that gave the village it's nickname. Some say it was because dolly tub repairers did good business as many local women took in washing. Another explanation may be that many men worked in the Pits and since there were no bathrooms the colliers used dolly tubs as baths. Yet another suggests it was called 'Dolly Tub City' because it was built in a hollow.

The bridge here, across the River Tonge is the division between Lever Bridge and Darcy Lever, the two are closely linked. To get a picture of how this part of the Tonge Valley looked in former days, take away the mills, the viaduct, the aqueduct , the church and the houses. In their place substitute a country mansion on the estate which is now part of Leverhulme Park and the lands on the opposite side of the river were the site of Darcy Lever Hall. The Hall was built in 1792, but it was recently demolished. Alan and his friends joined me as we arrive at the top of 'Hag End Brow' outside the 'Top Shop' with the local air raid shelter standing on the adjoining land. As we start the steady descent into the Tonge Valley with the imposing view of the viaduct before us, Alan turned to me and said, with some pride, **'Our Darcy Lever starts here"**.

Figure 34 Darcy Lever Viaduct

Opposite the 'Top Shop' is 'Lever Cottage' or number 2 Gatehouse to Bradford Park. As we reach the bottom of the brow, to our left stands the ornate St. Stephen and All Martyrs Church, known locally as 'Lever Bridge Church' because of it's proximity to the nearby bridge over the river, completed and consecrated in 1845 by the Bishop of Chester. The Church is built entirely of terra cotta clay from the Ladyshore pit at Little Lever and transported by barge along the nearby Manchester, Bolton and Bury Canal. The magnificent spire was influenced by the Cathedral at Freyberg in Germany and as at Freyberg, at the base of the spire was a light octagonal lantern again constructed of terra cotta the pediments and pinnacles of which covered the base of the spire. However, after some years the delicate fretwork of terra cotta began to crumble and sadly in 1939 the spire was removed. The Church is affectionately known by local people as 'The Pot Church'.

Figure 35 St. Stephens, Lever Bridge

As we leave the Church and look west the valley is dominated by the viaduct which, as Alan pointed out is ideal for 'Jumpers' (suicides), a number have been recorded over the years. He added **'A leap from up there means certain death'.** Just across the road is the 'Lever Bridge' pub and to my left, opposite the pub is the long climb up the wide steps to 'Gorses Mount', leading to Leverhulme Park. It was here that Alan, Peter, John and Duncan said 'Goodbye'. They climbed the steps to the Park for, as they said 'A game of footy'. As they reached the top, they turned, waved and disappeared from view. I had made four new friends. Would I ever see them again?

This part of Darcy Lever is known as 'Damside' with 'Damside' Mill to my left. As I look around me I realize that this is a major junction, with the road, the river Tonge Weir cascading beneath me and the viaduct carrying the railway line towering above me. Just ahead is the Damside Aqueduct, over which the Manchester, Bury and Bolton Canal flows towards 'Nob End' and onto Salford. The canal will become more important in the later stages of the 'Matchsticks Journey'.

The Aqueduct is known locally as 'Wooden Bottoms' and on Monday morning 7th February, 1938, Arnold Davies, a young butcher's errand boy was making his way to work along the aqueduct when he noticed something floating in the water. On closer inspection he realized it was the body of a woman and immediately called for help. Joseph Openshaw, who was employed by the L.M.S. Railway to look after the canal heard the lad's cry and hurried to assist. He used a pole to recover the body from the water, then called the Police. The body was identified as that of thirty one year old Alice Aldred, a local girl who lived with her parents nearby. It was soon discovered that Alice was in a somewhat volatile relationship with Arthur Wyatt who was older than Alice and lived in 'Viking Street', Bolton. It was reported that the couple had been seen together on the previous evening at a number of pubs in Darcy Lever and there had been arguments, witnessed by Alice's neighbours throughout the evening. Wyatt was questioned about his movements on that Sunday evening and was subsequently arrested. A post mortem was carried out on Alice's body and it was found she had died as a result of asphyxiation through drowning. Wyatt was charged with her murder and after a long trial at Manchester Assizes the jury found him guilty, but with a strong recommendation for mercy. However, a date and time, Wednesday, 18th May, at 8.00 a.m. was fixed for his execution at Strangeways Goal, but six days before he was to go to the gallows it was announced that Wyatt's life had been spared and he was sentenced to life imprisonment.

Figure 36 A Lancashire Navvy

Work on the construction of the Manchester, Bury and Bolton Canal commenced in 1791. Gangs of navvies dug out the Canal in sections which were eventually joined up. Materials were moved by hundreds of men, wheelbarrows, horses and carts. The Canal took six years to complete and from it's basin at 'Nob End' it is a 'Y' shaped waterway with a four mile branch to Bury, a three mile branch to Bolton and a six and a half mile stretch to Salford. By the time the Canal was completed, many coal pits had been sunk along it's length, some with their own short canal branch to the pit loading wharf, others had short tram roads to the canal side, often gravity operated. As well as coal, canal traffic included lime, salt, pottery and building materials, such as timber, bricks and stone. In 1796, although the canal wasn't quite finished, a passenger packet boat service started from Church Wharf, the Bolton terminus at Church Bank, to Bury and Manchester. This ran for forty years until the opening of the Manchester to Bolton Railway.

It is said that at the time of the canals hey-day, it was possible to board a passenger barge at Church Wharf and journey to America without leaving the water.

We leave Darcy Lever behind following the canal to the left and the river to the right via Aqueduct Street and pass Raikes Bleachworks. It is at this point that the Tonge joins the River Croal. The source of both rivers is on the slopes of Winter Hill. The 'Tonge', starting as Deane Brook flowing down the east of Bolton and the 'Croal', starting as the River Douglas to the west, through Horwich and Lostock, where it becomes the 'Middlebrook'. Flowing towards Bolton beside the railway line from Bolton to Wigan and the main west coast line to Scotland.

Overlooking the Middlebrook, to our right, is St. Mary's, Deane Church, originally built in the 14th century as St. Meridew Chapel consisting of just a nave, a chancel and a western tower. It was extended in the 15th century when it became the Mother Church of the Ecclesiastical Parish of Deane. Beside the Church is a wooded valley, this is 'Deane Clough', the course of 'Church Brook', originally named 'Kirkbrooke' from the ancient Saxon language.

Figure 37 Deane Church

Above the path leading down 'Deane Clough' and directly below the church is a large crevice. This is said to be the entrance to the ancient 'Deane Tunnel' which generations of 'Deane Folk' are convinced has existed for hundreds of years, certainly since the church was built. It is said that the tunnel was an escape route for priests connecting 'Deane Church' and the original 'Bolton Parish Church', but the tunnel collapsed, probably through erosion many years ago. Although 'The Cave' is still large enough for local kids to hold Saturday night parties inside by the light of their 'Bike Lamps'.

Figure 38 Deane Clough

'Church Brook' flows down the valley to join the Middlebrook, where it becomes the 'River Croal', which, in the late 1800's and for the next 100 years, because of industrial and domestic waste pollution, as was the case with virtually all the previously tranquil and picturesque rivers of the North West, became so polluted it took fifty years to clean them, but they will never be the same again. It was reported in the 'Bolton Chronicle', 11th June,1853, at a meeting of the town's Sanitary Committee, a statement read:-

'The Committee has for a long time been aware of the difficulty of cleaning the river Croal' and when they took into account that parties brought before the Bench had been merely fined

2s.6d. for putting probably a hundred cart loads of cinders in the river, the difficulty became greater still. There were factories, foundries and bleachworks which emptied all their filth into the river and unless these cases could be more vigorously dealt with then heretofore it would be out of the power of the Sanitary Committee to do their duty. It was not the poor, but the rich who could afford to pay who put the cinders in the river, and therefore ought to be proceeded against. This pollution of the 'Croal' continued for generations.

One hundred years later, in the 1950's, an article appeared in the 'Bolton Evening News' regarding proposed improvements to the River Croal through Bolton. It reads:-

'It is many years since the River Croal was an unpolluted waterway flowing between orchards and high banks of luscious grass. Yet, if the Town Council approves a recommendation to spend £152,000 culverting and developing part of the Croal valley, some of the valley's former beauty may be recaptured. Perhaps it was a similar thought which led 'Jenny Beck' to ask, **"did angling and swimming ever take place in the River Croal and when was the river bed paved?".**

In 1859, the offensive conditions of the Croal led to requests that it's bed be paved. The Town Council agreed to proceed with the work and in 1864 paving began on the section of the river between Chorley Street and Church Wharf. This was the time of the 1860's cotton famine and the work had been authorised by various Corporation Committees for the unemployed. The work lasted for a number of years, during which the river bed was brick lined from Queen's Park to Burnden, making the Croal the first 'brick bed' river in the country.

An early undated, probably early 1800's postcard, recently discovered reads:-

'Bolton-le-Moors, the garden city of the north, advertises great attractions to visitors and anglers. It says 'will find capital sport in the Middlebrook, one of the finest trout streams in the Country. There are ample facilities for bathing in the virgin River Croal and swimming competitions are held weekly with the entrance to the river from Water Street and King Street'.

On 13th November, 1858, an article was published in the Bolton Chronicle titled *'Sanitary conditions of Bolton'.*

'The river Croal is one gigantic and unbroken nuisance in warm and dry seasons, generating as it does, on it's torpid and sinuous course through the most densely populated parts of the town, the foulest and most deadly miasmata. This monster grievance will have to be dealt with boldly, but with every legitimate regard to vested rights. Let it not, however, be forgotten that the most indefeasible of vested rights is that which is bountiful provience has conferred upon every man, woman and child the right of breathing an uncontaminated atmosphere'.

The Croal is now flowing through 'Queen's Park' which was opened in 1866, by Lord Bradford and named 'The Queen's

Park' in 1897 to commemorate Queen Victoria's Diamond Jubilee. In 1878, the 'Chadwick Natural History Museum' was built in the Park and later the landmark Bandstand was built close to the river Croal and opened in June, 1924. Four thousand people attended the opening ceremony. However, just months later the Bandstand had to be moved as during that summer the audience was being constantly bitten by mosquitoes from the river which is now heading towards Bolton Town Centre.

Leaving the Park behind, it is crossed by the 'Dobson Bridge', a lattice girder bridge named after and opened in March 1879 by Sir Benjamin Dobson, Mayor of Bolton 1894-1898. As the Croal flows east from the bridge it is overlooked from the left by the Bolton Royal Infirmary, adjoining Queen's Park as an eighty four bed hospital built in 1883.

By 1872, it was becoming obvious that the original Infirmary in Nelson Square was inadequate to fulfil the needs of the town's increasing population and plans were made for a new Infirmary to be built on land in Chorley Street. By 1876 the scheme had been costed at a minimum of £70,000. Donations were pledged by a number of local businessmen, notably John Musgrave. Further funds were raised by the newly formed 'Working Men's Committee'. Donations mounted and on 1st May, 1880, the cornerstone of the main building was laid by Mr. Musgrave of the local spinning family.

The following three years was a period of intense fund raising, money was even collected from mill gates on a Saturday, the workers 'Pay Day', hence the title that lasted for many years, 'Hospital Saturday'.

The new infirmary gradually took shape and it opened for it's first patients on 21st July, 1883, by Alderman J. Musgrave J.P. and prior to the opening ceremony the 'Hospital Saturday Committee' organized a parade through the town centre.

Nearly 1500 medical books were donated by Samuel Crompton's descendants.

In 1886, a laundry and mortuary were completed. The Infirmary continued to expand and by the end of that year over 3,600 patients had been treated.

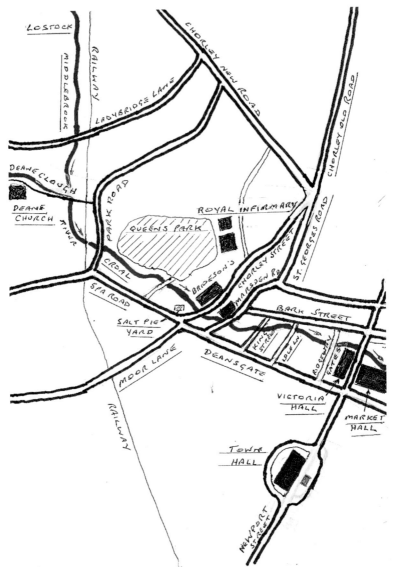

Map 7 River Croal, Lostock to the Town Centre

The Croal now flows towards Marsden Road, known locally as 'The High Level', officially opened in May 1877, by Alderman Peter Crook Marsden (hence the name). Previously just a wooden bridge spanned the Croal at this point, accessed by a narrow track leading down from Deansgate. The river continues under Chorley Street and the shops on 'White Lion Brow'. Hidden away, behind the shops and overlooking the Croal is 'Salt Pie Yard'. During the early 1800's, a 'Travelling Dentist' was a regular visitor to the yard, where he set up his chair and table on which he placed his ' instrument's. These were two pairs of rather large pliers, to be used for 'extractions'. He was accompanied by a three piece band, whose purpose was twofold. One was to play relaxing music to calm the prospective 'patients' down and once the dentist picked up his pliers, louder music was played to cover the screams of the terrified 'patients'.

The river now enters 'Exchange' Ward'. In the 1800's this was an area bounded by the 'Croal', Deansgate, Knowsley Street, Marsden Road and a warren of narrow streets. One such street was King Street which ran from Deansgate down to the Croal. In the early 1800's, number 17 King Street became a locally famous address. This was the workshop of Samuel Crompton, a man who became Bolton's most famous son, why? because Samuel Crompton, around 1779 invented the 'Spinning Mule', a machine that was to revolutionize the textile industry worldwide.

Figure 39 Samuel Crompton's house in King Street

Samuel was born in 1753, at 10 Firwood Fold, Bolton. The only son of George and Betty Crompton. His father was caretaker at 'Hall i'th ' Wood'. Samuel had two younger sisters. When he was just a boy his father George died suddenly leaving Samuel with the responsibility of helping his mother raise two little girls and contribute to the family resources. He learned to spin, a skill he mastered quickly, on James Hargreaves 'Spinning Jenny'. Samuel studied the 'Jenny' and was convinced he could invent something more efficient. He spent hours in his room in King Street working on his idea, in secret, for over five years. This absorbed all his spare time and money, including what he earned playing the violin at the Bolton Theatre.

Samuel's invention was originally known as the 'Mule Jenny' or the 'Hall i'th Wood wheel', from the name of his family home. The 'Jenny' later became known as the 'Spinning Mule', for which there was great demand. Samuel was a brilliant inventor but lacked marketing skills and depended on other manufacturers to finance him, so he never received the financial rewards to which he was entitled and other people benefitted from his lifetimes work. Samuel Crompton died in King Street on 26th June, 1827, aged 73 years and is buried in the Bolton parish church of St. Peter. Many years after his death a Memorial was erected and still stands in Nelson Square, Bolton.

Figure 40 Samuel Crompton

King Street was surrounded by alleyways and 'Courts' or 'Yards', such as 'Oliphant Court', 'Fogg's Court', 'Bambers Court' and many more, an area abundant in small workshops, stables, a timber yard and numerous small businesses. This was a town within a town, known locally as the 'Vagrants' Ward. From here business and domestic effluence poured into the already polluted Croal. In amongst all this activity, scores of kids lived and played there. They could play 'Hide and Seek' and because there were so many hiding places, they may not be found for hours, so, after a while they got 'fed up' and went home.

Alongside King Street, leading down to the river, is Central Street, originally named 'Water Street'. It was christened 'Idle Lane' by the locals and a 'gentleman' visiting the area is quoted as saying **"for there are none but idle scamps and vagabonds living there"**.

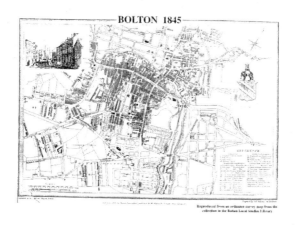

Figure 41 Bolton in 1845

In 1825, amongst this warren of narrow streets and alleyways, in 'Back King Street', an 'oasis of learning' was opened. This was the 'Mechanics Institute', the aim of which was to moralize the working classes by combining instruction with amusement. The objective was to provide rooms, a library, lectures and evening classes to encourage the working men to educate themselves, particularly technical subjects that could help them in their work. However, it soon became apparent to the well meaning, middle class 'Honorary Members', that the workers, after a ten hour shift at the factory or mill, preferred the company and atmosphere of the 'Kings Arms' round the corner.

Close to the Institute, in Kingsgate, is a building of some mystery. Ornately carved in a stone 'Mullion' above the entrance are carved the words 'Casual Ward', giving the impression that this was possibly a small 'Infirmary'. But in 1911, it was listed as 'Bolton Union Vagrant Ward' under it's supervisor Mr. A.G. Bland. The building has also been described in the local press as 'A monument to the age of Dickens'. Built in the early 1800's it has a history of poverty and depression, which reached it's peak at the end of the 1800's.

Tramps, penniless travellers and 'down and outs' stayed the night in return for a day's labour chopping wood.

'It was seen as a haven for the poor, a salvation of the middle class Victorian conscience'. In other words, a Victorian 'Doss House'.

A number of bridges spanned the Croal along this section, notably a substantial and quite ornate cast iron structure at the bottom of Central Street named locally as 'Mick Buck's Bridge' identified by a large 'Mick Buck, Bolton' casting on the support girder. Messrs. Buck and Son had a foundry in Turton Street and during the time of the Boer Wars, it was reported in the Bolton Journal that two Bolton men, Miles and Stephen Buck, relatives of Michael Buck had been accused by the Military of spying for the 'Boers'. These accusations were later found to be totally untrue and the brothers were exonerated.

Figure 42 Mick Buck's Bridge

The local kids playground stretched along the Croal from here down to Church Bank and the canal at 'Church Wharf'. From this point the canal and the Croal run parallel. Some of them fished for pike from the Jetty beside the boathouse from where, in the 1800's the packet boats left for Manchester and beyond.

We follow the Croal as it flows under Knowsley Street, to the right is the rear wall of the 'Victoria Hall'. As I look up at the wall I realize that there are a number of datestones, one of which is carved 'Laid by Thomas Walker J.P. May 5[th,] 1898', this and three other datestones, all 1898, are set in decorative panels made up of sixty three bricks, each brick is individually numbered in numerical order. This is fascinating. I ask myself, what is the significance of four panels of sixty three and one panel of one hundred and ninety one, totalling three hundred and seventy two individually numbered bricks, all in numerical order. Why has someone gone to all this trouble and effort to create what I consider to be a highly decorative piece of masonry on the back wall of the Victoria Hall, facing the river Croal, were no one can see it? There must be a logical answer. I can only assume that the bricks had probably been sponsored to raise funds for the building of the Hall. In the late 1800's Brook Street which is overlooked by the 'Memorial Panels', including the bricks, would have been a busy thoroughfare with people and horse drawn traffic passing constantly.

Figure 43 A panel of Victoria Hall "bricks"

The Victoria Hall Methodist Mission was financed by Mr. Thomas Walker J.P. and completed in 1898 followed by a lavish opening ceremony in 1901, attended by many local dignitaries. It was known as the 'Walker Building' and is built on the site of an old graveyard adjoining the 'Ridgeway Gates Chapel', opened by John Wesley in 1777 and recently demolished.

The original idea behind the Victoria Hall project, was it would be a modern concept of Methodism. It was built to be more like a theatre, with a horseshoe balcony, making it more inviting to the ordinary man, rather than a traditional church. 'Victoria Hall' was to be a place of sanctuary from alcohol abuse, the biggest cause of violent crime in the 19th century, unemployment and depravation. A 'Penny Concert' with a music hall atmosphere and live variety acts or a silent film was shown on Saturday night with an invitation to come to worship on Sunday morning. The strategy worked, many people turned up regularly on Sunday morning.

The 'Walker Memorial Hall' was added to in 1935 and another donation funded the building of the ninety foot high terra cotta tower. It was said the tower is 'One of the finest in Methodism rose in halls complete'.

During both World Wars the Hall had a vital role as an Air Raid Warden Post.

Figure 44 Opening of the Victoria Hall

Figure 45 Brook Street steps to the left.

As we emerge on the other side of Knowsley Street, to the right is a flight of stone steps leading up to the street above and the site of one of Bolton's most iconic buildings, the magnificent 'Market Hall'. A building which, during it's construction generated interest throughout the town. One of the new market's modern features was the latest heating system fuelled by coal fired furnaces and during the first ten years after construction, until the Croal bed was paved, coal for the furnaces was transported by flat bottomed boats up the Croal from the canal at Church Wharf. Boltonians couldn't wait to see it finished. It was completed in 1855 and an article appeared in the Bolton Chronicle on 22nd December, 1855 headed:-

Opening of Bolton New Market Hall

'No building can rival in taste and architectural display. The new and splendid Market Hall, whose public opening we record below, crowns all other local landmarks with classic purity and magnificence. In point of utility no building ever supplied greater public want. While as an ornament to the town it stands unsurpassed.'

'The Opening Ceremony'

'At an early hour on Wednesday morning the sounds of the church bells pealed merrily through the air and flags which floated from all the buildings and many of the shops in the principal streets indicated that the day was to be one of general rejoicing. The weather was all that could be desired.
A number of shops were wholly and others partially closed and some of the mills and workshops ceased working early to allow such hands as were desirous of joining in the public procession, in honour of the opening, an opportunity of doing so. The various societies and bands of music intending to join in the procession began to form near the Borough Court at twelve o' clock'.

'The Market Hall by Gaslight'

'The Market Hall was crowded with people from soon after six o' clock to ten o' clock. It was brilliantly lit up. The Gilnow Saxhorn Band occupied the platform. Many people had gone there in the hope of enjoying a dance, but the building was so crowded that dancing was out of the question.

A grand ball in celebration of the opening was held in the evening at the Bath's Assembly Rooms and was attended by the elite of the town and neighbourhood.

The first market in the hall was held on Saturday and it being the Christmas market there was an excellent show of all descriptions of poultry.

The Butchers soon disposed of their choice cuts at seven pence, halfpenny a pound. The show of Christmas geese was very meagre, but such as were in the market sold readily at Eightpence a pound. At night the hall was so crowded that the avenues were almost impassable and during this time several pockets were picked'.

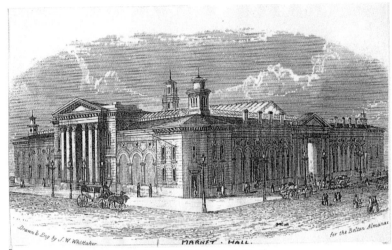

Figure 46 Market Hall

Figure 47 Interior of the Market Hall

Ten years later, in 1865, a new fish market was built in a similar gothic style, adjacent to the Market Hall, on Bridge Street, which thrived for over sixty years until the late 1920's when the building was deteriorating and becoming unhygienic. It was decided to replace it with a new, modern Fish Market in Ashburner Street. The old market, standing by 'The Croal' was closed in 1932 and demolished later that year.

On the night before actual demolition started a police sergeant was patrolling a practically deserted 'Bridge Street' when he heard a strange 'chattering' sound and looking behind him towards the fish market he saw what he described as a 'wall of rats' leaving the old building and heading straight towards him. His first reaction was to jump onto the nearest shop window ledge and hang on for 'dear life' as the 'chattering mass' swarmed by. He was adamant they were led by a huge 'king rat' heading round the corner into 'Bow Street'

The rat story doesn't end there. The witness is convinced that this incident was only a 'rehearsal' for the events that were to happen the following night, when, at about the same time, around 11.00 p.m. in the same place, Frank, an experienced tram driver over many years, was to witness a unique event in Bolton's history.

The following is based on his recollection of the incident:-

"I only ever saw him in a hurry that once" said Frank who goes onto describe 'Paddy' (we'll assume he was Irish) who, at the time was the town's best known 'Bobby'. He was a veritable giant. He had been a fighter in his younger days and was getting on for eighteen stone but not as tough as he looked. He was, deep down, a 'big softy' and numerous tales were told in the town of the many good turns 'Paddy' did for those in need. As well as his size he had an authority about him generating a certain respect within the community.

"I never saw him get a move on" said Frank who goes on to say, **"It was late on the night the demolition of the fish market started, I saw the most terrifying thing I have seen in all my years driving trams, I'll never forget it. I was driving the last tram from Tonge Moor, there were no passengers on board, just me and 'the guard'. It was about eleven o' clock. As I headed up 'Bow Street', I saw the large, uniformed figure of 'Paddy' running towards me from 'Bridge Street'. He held up his hand and stopped in front of the tram waving furiously. I put the brake on fast. You don't question Paddy. I wondered what had made him run so fast. He jumped on the platform beside me shouting 'Jaysus', 'Mary and Joseph', Frank, for god's sake get up them bloody stairs quick and tell the guard to get up them back stairs, the rats are coming.** In all the commotion I asked what all the fuss was about, as he literally pushed me up the stairs. As we reached the 'top deck', he turned me round and pointed towards 'Bridge Street'.

Pouring round the corner, like a flood of dark water, came thousands of rats, their evil eyes reflected in the trams lights. We had met them 'head on'. **"Keep still and say your bloody prayers"** shouted Paddy, or they'll have us. As they reached the tram the flood parted by us on both sides. True or not, people believe that when threatened, rats will go for your throat.

As they passed I noticed that they were well organized, led by the biggest rats, forming a guard around the flanks. These were fearsome looking creatures, as big as cats. Some seemed to be heavily scarred, probably from old fights. Their numbers increased, there must have been several thousand of them filling 'Bow Street' from end to end. They streamed by for what seemed like an eternity during which we hardly dared draw a breath. I thought **"will I get home to-night"?,** as we saw the rearguard, again led by the 'king rats' sweep past us. Thank god none of them had tried to enter the tram.

We heard later that as they reached the bottom of 'Bow Street', they poured into the culverts in 'Bank Street' and into the 'Croal', from where they had come, under the fish market.

We had just witnessed a veritable 'exodus of rats'.

Another rat of some note at the time, resided just round the corner from 'Bow Street' in 'All Saints Street'. This was 'Ernie' the 'Co-operative Society Slaughterhouse' rat. He was described as 'bigger than a tom cat', having been 'weaned' on 'offal' by his friend 'Tiny', a giant slaughter man, who was described by his workmates as 'A match for any animal that fought back'. Sadly, after a hard day's work, 'Tiny' was found dead among a pile of animal parts, watched over by 'Ernie' the rat

After a post mortem, it was announced that 'Tiny' was unmarked and had died from natural causes. After his death 'Ernie' was never seen again.

The 'Croal' continues to flow south east towards Church Bank and the Parish Church. Along here it passes under Crown Street leading to Churchgate, probably the oldest and still the busiest part of 'Little Bolton'.

It is in this area that 'Parson Folds', a popular local clergyman was regularly seen in friendly conversation with the local people. The Rev. James Folds was born in Upper Darwen in 1728 and moved to Bolton as a young clergyman in the early 1750's. James was a man of many parts loved and respected by both the rich and poor of the town. He soon became affectionately known as 'Parson Folds'.

He became 'Lecturer of Bolton' in 1755, a position he held until his death. He was a prosperous man and had properties in various parts of the town. Despite his wealth he was a 'Peoples Clergyman' and to write of 'Parson Folds' without recounting some of the stories relating to him would be unthinkable.

The Parson was described as 'a little eccentric'. He officially preached at Turton Church. Every Sunday morning he rode his horse to Turton making impromptu stops along the way, 'spreading the word' to the non converted. He was regularly seen mixing and socializing with people around the town centre, it was common knowledge that Parson Folds was partial to an odd glass of rum. He would travel regularly to Liverpool

Docks on his friend's horse and cart to pick up his 'Jamaica Rum', sitting astride the barrel on his way back to Bolton.

The Parson employed a local man as his personal servant and named him 'Sorry'. Both the man's true name and the reason the Parson named him 'Sorry' is a mystery. On one occasion 'Sorry' was asked to order a 'Chaisse' (a horse and carriage) to pick up the Parson at the 'Swan', on Bradshawgate, one of his regular 'Watering Holes'. 'Sorry' informed the driver he would be carrying the 'Lecturer of Bolton', the 'Curate of Walmsley' and the 'Rector of West Hythe', all three titles held by Folds. On arriving at the 'Swan' the 'Lecturer' took his seat in the 'Chaisse' and the driver continued to wait. When asked by the Parson **"Why are you waiting?"**, the driver replied **"I'm awaiting the other two gentlemen"**. **"Drive on"** said the Parson, **I'm like the Holy Trinity - three in one"**.

One day in the 'Cross Guns' at Egerton, another of his favourite Hostelries, quietly enjoying his favourite glass of rum, he was approached by a parishioner, who suggested that with three such esteemed titles he must be making a fortune and asked **'How much ar't worth Parson?.** Leaning forward confidentially the Parson whispered **'con't keep a secret lad?'.** **'Aye',** the man replied. **'an so can I'** said Folds.

Probably the most amusing 'of the many 'Parson Folds' stories is said to have occurred when the cellar of his house in Fold Street needed paving and asked a local tradesman for a price to do the job. A few days later the man returned with what he thought was a fair price which he conveyed to the Parson, who was aghast at the price quoted and responded by saying **'See lad, i'll tak' thi' wheer tha' can get 'em for nowt''**. The Parson then led the workman across the Parish Church graveyard and directed him to remove a number of the more ancient stones from the oldest graves. It is said that when the house was demolished, some years later, to be replaced by a barber's shop, the flagstones still remained bearing traces of the original inscriptions.

In the late 1700's, Parson Folds organized and participated in the early games of 'street football' through Bolton town centre. Teams of up to fifty young men wearing brass tipped clogs, which could and often did do serious damage to opponents, surged along the banks of the Croal, kicking a primitive leather ball from 'one goal' in the Bank Street area to another 'goal' near Brideson's Bleachworks in Chorley Street. The ball spending more time in the Croal than on the street. However in 1791, after complaints by local residents the 'County Court' deemed that the game was a 'serious breach of the peace'. This had little effect and by the time of Parson Folds death in 1820 organized football matches were attracting large crowds of spectators.

Folds died, still bearing the title 'Lecturer of Bolton' in 1820 at the age of 92. To the last he was a familiar figure, supported by his two walking sticks, inching his way to his final home at 'Sweet Green House' in Crook Street. - 'A Bolton Legend'.

Again reported in the Bolton Chronicle dated 17th July, 1852 :-

'Destruction of the Star Concert Room by fire"

The building known as the 'Star Concert Rooms and Museum' was destroyed in the course of Tuesday night, when it became the scene of one of the most alarming fires that have taken place in the Borough for some years.

'The 'Star Concert Room and Museum' as our readers are aware, has, for a considerable period, formed a point of attraction to thousands of the inhabitants of Bolton and the neighbourhood, who have resorted thither more or less frequently for the purpose of amusement and recreation. Entertainment having been provided ever varying and of a character which always drew interested and admiring audiences, and the destruction of the premises by fire will be remembered perhaps equally in consequence of the amount of property devoured and the fact of that property embracing a very notable establishment.'

The building was erected a little more than twelve years ago by Mr. Thomas Sharples, then of the Millstone Tavern, Crown Street, who subsequently occupied it in connection with the 'Star Inn', a public house in Churchgate, previously called the 'Cock Inn'. It stood immediately behind the 'Star' and was in three general divisions or storeys, the first on the ground floor, used for the purposes of brewhouse, stable yard, paint shop, workshops etc., the second the concert room and the third the museum. Above the museum was a promenade, forming in great measure the roof of the building, the south end being distinguished by the mast of a large ship, with a quantity of rigging.

The great object of attraction was the Concert Room, an apartment extending the whole length and breadth of the building, with galleries at the side and north end and a theatre stage at the south end. The Concert Room was laid out with seats and drinking tables and under the end gallery was a Bar from which ale, spirits and refreshments were retailed to visitors. The entertainments provided in this part of the establishment were on the weekday evenings, Monday afternoon and at pastimes during the whole day and comprised music, comic and sentimental singing, living tableaux etc, etc.

The museum extended over the Concert Room, from which it was approached by a long flight of stairs. Many objects of a rare and curious character were displayed in the museum, which was open to inspection at all hours of the day. Amongst the collection was a number of wax figures, models, sundry views, pictures, stuffed reptiles and birds, geological specimens, busts, moving mechanical figures, living monkeys etc.

In the museum also, on the right of the entrance, is Mr. J Benfold's 'Temple of Magic'. Mr. Benfold kept on hand, as the catalogue stated, apparatus for playing deceptive, but pleasing experiments, the use of which might be taught to such as would become purchasers. The same gentleman had also rooms on the promenade for taking photographic portraits.

The promenade was considerably narrower than the Concert Room owing to the slanting roof on each side of the museum. It was floored with timber laid upon lead, with fence railings at the ends and sides and on fine days people would often spend an hour or two in viewing thence the town and country. An artificial pond formed of an iron cistern was placed at the north end, behind which were two prominent objects in the shape of representations of a 'Cherokee Indian' and a colossal female figure from a ship named 'Phoebus'.

Here then was a large building in the middle of a spot thickly studded with cottages, shops, inns and other erections, embracing all the property within the south side of Churchgate.

The one building that incredibly escaped the raging inferno was the nearby Bank Street Unitarian Chapel. A gothic stronghold of Methodism surrounded by establishments providing all forms of 'Entertainment'. Erected in the 1700's and described as a 'venerable building' standing on 'Windy Bank', which was originally the site of the town dungeon. The chapel stood on this site until 1856, when it was replaced by a new chapel, built of local stone from 'Horrocks Fold' Quarry.

In 1874, a Sunday School was added. Two pubs, the 'Seven Stars' and the 'Bank Inn', a house and a shop were bought and demolished. The school was then built on the site. The 'Seven Stars' had been used as a temporary school from 1866.

Bert Jones, a local historian, after a visit to the chapel writes:-

'The history of 'Bank Street' mirrors the changes that took place in the town. The 17th Century founders were landowners and merchants, representative of the time. Followed in the 18th Century, by the pioneers of the industrial revolution. In the 19th Century and early 20th Century, the mill owning families are well represented. Names like Harwood, Haslam, Haseldon, Crook, Heywood and Darbyshire, Taylor and Thomasson.

With the growth of the town and the creation of the borough, many members of these families entered public life, as M.P's, J.P's and Councillors. Charles James Darbyshire and Robert Heywood were, respectively the first and second Mayor's of Bolton in 1838 and 1839. All these families made generous donations to the town.

Leading off Bank Street by the Croal is 'Manor Street', where in the 1860's a wholesale grocer, James Lever, owned a warehouse. At that time his son, William Hesketh Lever began his working life here, where he developed the first 'Sunlight Soap'. Young William was, many years later to become 'Lord Lever', who built the famous 'Port Sunlight'.

As the Croal flows down Churchgate it takes a change of direction towards the west, passing 'Church Wharf' and the Bolton, Bury and Manchester canal. Standing by the wharf is a boathouse and the 'Bull and Wharf ' pub, probably built to coincide with the building of the canal in 1791. This was the terminus for all canal traffic leaving Bolton for Bury, Salford and Manchester. Completed in 1805, at a total cost of £127,700.

The journey by packet boat from here to Manchester took approximately three hours.

Figure 48 Church Wharf

In the mid 1800's the pub nicknamed the 'Boat House' was always kept busy as an average of 20,000 people per year started or ended their journey here at the wharf, which along with this stretch of the canal closed in 1941.

High above the wharf, to the right is the tower of the Parish Church of St. Peter, Bolton-le-Moors *(Bolton Parish Church)*. This is a magnificent example of the Victorian gothic style church and is the third known building to have occupied the same commanding site. Fragments of stone from Saxon and Norman times are all that remain of the earliest buildings. These can be seen in the museum corner of the church, which was opened in 1871, replacing the 15th Century predecessor which had fallen into disrepair. The cost of the new Church, £45,000 was met entirely by Peter Ormerod, a wealthy Cotton Manufacturer and Banker. The Church was designed by the Lancaster based Architect E.J. Paley of Paley and Austin.

Figure 49 Bolton Parish church

Built of Longridge stone, the Church is 156ft. from east to west, 67 ft. wide and 82ft. high. The spaciousness of the interior has been enhanced by the removal of superfluous pews. The tower, said to be the loftiest in Lancashire, is over 180ft. high and commands extensive views of the surrounding moorlands from which the old title 'Bolton-le-Moors' originates. It's fourteen bells have peeled down the centuries, calling people to worship as well as marking both joyful and sad local and national events.

The growth of the town in the middle ages is reflected in the 'Grant of Right' to hold a market in 1251 and a Charter of 'Enfranchisement' granted in 1253. Around 1420 a new Church was built, typical of the squat, solid structures commonly to be found in this part of the country. The mark of it's 17th Century history still rests in Bolton, as a stronghold of puritanisme. The town was besieged three times during the Civil War and as a consequence of the so called 'Massacre' of 1644 by the Royalist Forces under Prince Rupert and Lord Derby. The names of seventy eight soldiers are recorded in the register of burials. In subsequent reprisals Lord Derby was beheaded at the Market Cross in Churchgate. The 'Okey' tombstone, sited outside the south wall of the Church, gives a plaintive and exaggerated account of those disturbed days. The Churchyard closed for burials in 1855. It contains many monuments, amongst them, those of Samuel Crompton, Benjamin Hick, Dr. Samuel Chadwick and many other respected citizens of the town.

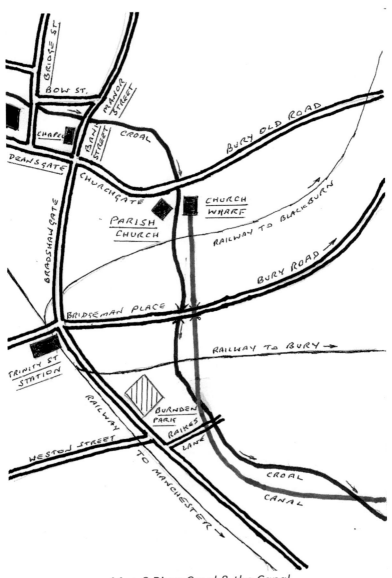

Map 8 River Croal & the Canal

The Croal and the Canal now flow side by side towards 'Burnden'. Dominating this community is 'Burnden Park', the home of Bolton Wanderers. It was here quite recently in March 1946, thirty three people died when, it is estimated that over 85,000 people were packed into Burnden Park to watch Bolton Wanderers play Stoke City in an F.A. Cup 5th Round replay. Remembered by many Bolton people but often referred to as 'The Forgotten Football Disaster'. As well as those killed, over 500 people were injured, some seriously.

Figure 50 Burnden Disaster

On that fateful Saturday, my Grandad, Bill Peters (affectionately known by my sister and I as 'Grandpa Peters') an avid Bolton supporter, left his home in Rushey Fold Lane, Halliwell, for his much awaited afternoon at the 'Match', which that day was an early kick off. No floodlights in 1946. He walked down the lane to the tram stop outside Mr. Fletcher's Toffee Shop on Halliwell Road to catch the one o'clock tram to town. This was only the second stop from the start of it's journey but it was almost full, a sign of things to come? He got off the tram at the terminus on 'Station Brew', directly opposite Trinity Street Railway Station and joined the crowd of people heading to 'Burnden'. As they reached Manchester Road more people joined the throng coming from Bradshawgate. Grandpa, who was a big man, soon found himself being carried along by the sea of tightly packed bodies. Using his strength Grandpa managed to break free from the crowd and found himself stood on the steps of Bolton Technical College. He gathered his thoughts, lit his pipe and as he stood looking down on the thousands of people heading towards 'Burnden', he thought **"If it's like this here, what's it going to be like at the ground"?,** but he hadn't missed a home match in years and he certainly wasn't going to miss this one. He decided to re-join the throng and was soon outside the ground where the crowd were herded away from the 'Embankment' entrances, from where he normally watched the match and was obviously, by now over it's capacity. The crowd was directed to the 'Great Lever End' which he hoped would be less crowded and he would have a better chance of at least seeing the match.

Even before 'Kick Off', during the friendly banter between the rival supporters, there was concern about the numbers on the 'Embankment' end. From his position Grandpa could see the crowd swaying to and fro. He could see people climbing over the fence from the railway line which passed behind the embankment. This added to the numbers putting further pressure on the spectators below. He managed to watch the match for a few minutes, watching the 'mesmerising dribbles' of the legendary Stoke Winger, Stanley Matthews (later to become 'Sir Stanley'), but his attention was again directed to the embankment opposite, where he could see that many people were in trouble.

Women and children were being passed over the heads of an estimated 25,000 people on the 'Embankment' to the safety of the Pitch, where bodies, with their faces covered were already laid on the grass. The overall pressure of bodies was such, that a number of steel barriers collapsed causing an avalanche of people falling onto others who were crushed to death. The game was stopped for a short time, during which Grandpa could see people being carried away on stretchers, but he, like thousands of others, certainly at the 'Lever End', where he stood, didn't realize at the time, just how many people had died.

I, as an eight year old in 1946 vividly remember that Saturday afternoon. I was playing with my Cousin Gerrard, who lived just off School Hill, when we heard the bells of approaching Ambulances coming from town. Gerrard said **"I'll bet the're goin ter't morgue, come on"**. I followed him round the corner and we stood at the end of 'Concertina Row' facing the Mortuary on School Hill and watched the Ambulances and Police Cars drive through the gates. A crowd soon gathered, not realizing what had just happened at 'Burnden'. Suddenly my friend Brenda (Buzzer) Bee arrived shouting **"Ay (my** nickname) your **Mam says you have to come home now".** I wasn't keen on leaving the excitement outside the Morgue but Buzzer insisted. We both ran up Tyndall Street to our home in Center Street where 'Mam' was waiting with my sister Sandra. Mam was very upset and said **"We're going to Grandpa's house, there has been some trouble at Burnden Park and Grandpa is there".** She had heard on the radio that people had died. We soon arrived at Grandpa's house where Mam's sisters, my aunties Hilda and Edith were stood outside sick with worry, looking down Rushey Fold Lane towards Halliwell Road. Most of the neighbours, including Clarice Crabtree, who's husband Harry was also at the Match, stood waiting apprehensively for the next tram to arrive from town, hopefully bringing our loved ones safely home. The tram came and went, we waited. Then both Grandpa and Harry appeared together at the bottom of the street. We all rushed to greet them. There were hugs and some kisses. They were both taken by surprise. They didn't at the time, realize the extent of the tragedy that had happened a couple of hours before. Our loved ones were home safe, but thirty three families couldn't welcome their loved ones home that Saturday.

Just a few days later the mayor of Bolton opened a Relief Fund which was swelled by numerous
Charity Football Matches, including England versus Scotland at Maine Road, Manchester. The Fund raised almost £40,000 for the victims relatives. The enquiry that followed found that the crowd had unwittingly been responsible for it's own fate, and that no blame could be attached to anyone. However, a series of recommendations relating to the reception and control of

crowds at the grounds in the Football League was put forward, limiting crowd numbers at each individual ground.

From Burnden the Croal enters the 'Raikes Valley' and beside the river, 'Raikes Clough' a picturesque part of the valley popular with the local people, continues to the 'Raikes Bleachworks' where it is joined, from the left by the Tonge. The Croal continues south, flowing past Great Lever Chemical Works at 'Bull Hill', then under Farnworth Bridge carrying the main road from 'Moses Gate' to Little Lever. At this point I ask the question **"How does the term 'Moses Gate' originate"?** It is a corruption of the two words, first 'Mosses', meaning peaty or marshland and secondly, the old English word 'Gata' meaning a way, street or road, together meaning 'The way across the moss'. The two words are found in other local names, such as 'Kearsley Moss' and 'Clifton Moss', also Bolton street names such as 'Churchgate' and 'Deansgate', meaning the way to Church or Deane.

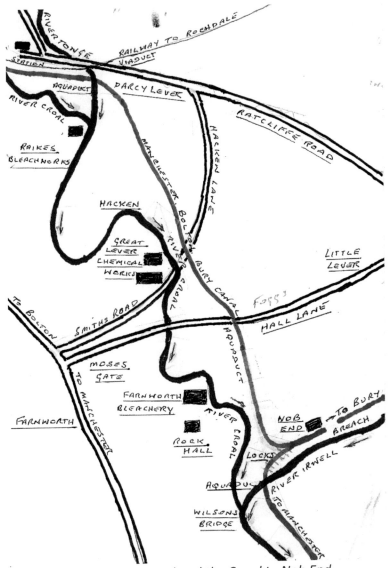

Map 9 River Croal and the Canal to Nob End

From here the Croal and the canal flow virtually side by side, as the aqueduct carries the canal over the road and onto 'Nob End'. The river continues past Farnworth Paper Mill, dating back to 1674, founded and run by generations of the Crompton family. The Founder, Robert Crompton was once described as 'The first in a long line of men of paper'. To our right is 'Rock Hall', built in 1807 by Thomas Bonsor Crompton, however he preferred to live at nearby 'Vale House'.

After Crompton's death in 1883, paper production at the Mill ended. Some years later in1894 it re-opened as the 'Farnworth Bleachery' until it finally closed in the 1930's.

From this point the area bordering the Croal and Irwell Valley is riddled with mine workings, from shallow pits to deep shafts. One such Pit was 'Fogg's Pit', standing to our left, beside the canal. The Pit was sunk in the 1820's by Andrew Knowles and was very successful, reaching the peak of it's production during the 1830s. However, Pit accidents were a common occurrence during the 1800's and Fogg's was no exception.

In February, 1877, a fire started deep in the mine workings, most of the miners escaped, but the fire spread quickly, creating a huge amount of smoke, suffocating ten men. Rescuers were hampered by the smoke along with the escaping methane gas, causing a huge explosion. The rescue attempt was aborted. Some days later the bodies were recovered and the Pit re-opened.

Thirty years later, in 1907, tragedy struck at Fogg's again, when, in number one shaft, an ascending cage, carrying ten men to the surface, collided with a descending cage, causing the former to crash to the bottom of the shaft, killing all ten men in the cage. Fogg's closed in 1912. The 'Croal' flows on to 'Wilson's bridge'. It is here the Croal meets the River Irwell flowing from the east, past Creams Paper Mill in Little Lever. The 'Creams' site was established in 1776 by the then owner, Adam Crompton as the 'old enclosed homestead and Paper Mill and Drying House'. In his Will in 1791 he refers to *'The estate where I now dwell',* commonly called or known by the name of 'Creams' which is still one of the largest employers in the area.

Figure 51 Fogg's Pit

Close by, bordering the canal is 'Ladyshore colliery' owned by the Fletcher family. Most of the pit was worked beneath the Irwell and on Friday, 10th July, 1835, one of the miners unwittingly cut through the roof of a gallery and thousands of gallons of water from the river above rushed into the mine and within minutes seventeen men and boys were drowned.

News of the tragedy soon spread throughout 'Little Lever'. Over that weekend people flocked to the Pit for news of their loved ones and by Sunday afternoon the 'Manchester Guardian' reported that thousands of people waited at the Pit Head for news of the missing miners, but three weeks later three bodies still hadn't been recovered. It was later reported, after an enquiry that the river bed and the colliery roof were separated by only two or three feet at the point where the river had broken through.

'Ladyshore' also gave it's name to boat building on the nearby canal and in the early 1800's the Ladyshore Coal Company Yard at Little Lever was actively involved in building special canal boats. These were the 'Ice Boats'. Whatever time of the year, summer or winter coal and goods had to be moved and in the winter this was achieved by special men in special boats. In rain, biting winds, snow and fog, men coped without much difficulty. However, ice on the canal was a totally different matter, even a thin skin of ice could cut through the hull of most canal boats. But the specially built 'Ice Boats', were shorter in length and narrower in width than the standard boat making them much more sturdy. The outside of the hull was covered in iron sheeting. The boats were forty five feet long and four feet, six inches wide. The boats were horse drawn by up to four horses, depending on the thickness of the ice and manned by four men who literally 'rocked the boat' from side to side thus creating a surge in the water, propelling the boat forward and cracking the ice ahead. This procedure continued throughout the day until they returned to the Ladyshore Ice Boat Berth and on home. These were, indeed, 'hard men'.

'Nob End' was, in the 1800's a busy junction from Bolton in the west and Bury in the east to travel on to Salford and Manchester. Overlooking the canal is the local Pub, the 'Nob Inn', previously known locally as the 'Boathouse'. It was always kept busy serving boat passengers nipping in for a quick drink to refresh themselves for the rest of their journey. The 'Nob Inn' overlooked 'Prestolee Locks', these were 'Staircase' locks leading down from the higher level 'Bolton, Bury Canal' to the lower level, some eighty five feet below Manchester and Salford branch. This flight was built as two sets of three locks with a very short distance between the two sets, making six locks in all. A steep cobbled footpath, covered by a wooden roof ran alongside the locks. Passengers disembarked from the Bolton or Bury packet boats and walked along the covered path to join another boat waiting to take them on the next stretch to Salford and Manchester. This saved the time needed for a boat to negotiate the locks and also helped to conserve water.

Figure 52 Nob Inn

Just to the east of the locks, on the Bury stretch, a serious breach on the south side of the canal occurred in June 1936. It is said, on that day, a miner from Ladyshore had just finished his shift and was pedalling his bike along the canal towpath, when he heard a 'cracking' sound behind him, he turned and to his horror, the towpath was breaking up behind him. He couldn't believe what he was seeing and realized he had to get away quickly and pedalled 'Hell for Leather' towards 'Nob End' as the whole hillside supporting the canal collapsed sending millions of gallons of water crashing down to the Irwell some one hundred feet below. Luckily the miner escaped unharmed. A passing Day Boat was sucked into the breach and was left hanging precariously over the sheer drop. The breach was never repaired as, at the time, it was deemed not to be cost effective as the amount of canal traffic was declining as movement of goods was switching to the railways. The canal still remains dry from 'Creams' to 'Nob End'.

Figure 53 The 1936 breach

During the 1800's, the 'Day Boat' was the most common boat on the Bolton Bury canal, carrying coal from the Collieries in the area. However, on other local canals, there was the occasional horse drawn 'Family Boat'. These were owned by a boatman who lived and worked on his boat with his wife and children all year round. Others would be joined by their families for just a few weeks depending on how far the boat had to travel to deliver it's cargo. Overcrowding was a common problem, with some of these boats having a small cabin fore and aft and would often carry the boatman, his wife and up to seven children, many of whom had been born on the boat.

Once the cargo had been loaded on board there was very little space for the children who slept 'Nose to Tail' in their beds. The boatman's wife did her normal chores, cooking, washing etc., but also helped with steering the boat and helped the older children or 'Nippers' drive the horses along the towpath hauling the heavy boat with it's cargo behind them. These 'Boat Horses' were treated just like one of the family. It is said that in the late 1800's on the Rochdale canal 'Rob', a boat horse, towing the family boat fell from the towpath into a Lock and despite the family's efforts to save him, drowned in the Lock. The family were devastated.

The work done by his wife and children meant that the boatman didn't have to employ a mate, thus saving the family money. Most of these families took great pride in their boats, which were treated just like any home, kept as clean as possible depending on the nature of the cargo. The horses were well fed, well shod and stood proud with their brasses highly polished.

This outdoor life kept the boat people relatively free from infectious diseases, even though sanitation was a problem. There were no toilet facilities on the boat, so the men and women simply went behind the nearest hedge. If the family ran out of fresh water, they used the water from the canal for washing and even drinking. Washing was usually done using a tub on the towpath. However, mortality was high amongst these people, accidents, especially drownings were common place among the younger children. In fact some boatmen actually tethered their children to the deck to stop them wandering off and falling into the canal. Often the older children, driving the horses were kicked and some were badly injured. Life on the canal was hard but probably no worse than that of an average working family in the Mills and Factories of the nearby towns.

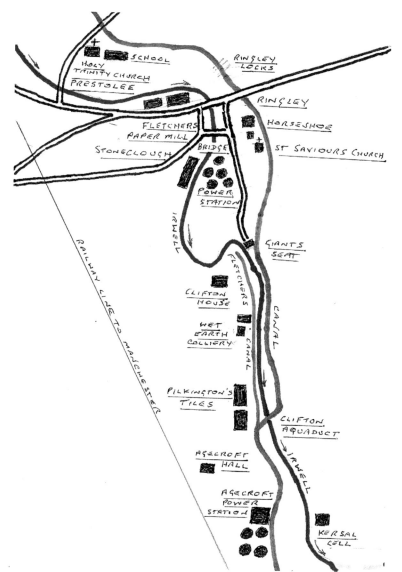

Map 10 River Irwell and the Canal to Agecroft

Leaving 'Prestolee Locks' and 'Nob End' behind, the Irwell and the canal flow south towards the community of Prestolee, dominated by the impressive 'Holy Trinity' church and the adjacent primary school which was opened in September 1911 as 'Outwood and Kearsley' Council School. Almost two hundred and fifty pupils attended, crammed into four classrooms, over sixty pupils per room. Initially the school did not have a good reputation. However in 1918 twenty eight years old Mr. Edward F. O'Neil was appointed headmaster, the youngest head teacher ever to be appointed in Lancashire. The reason for O'Neil's (later to be affectionately known throughout the community as 'Teddy O'Neil') were his controversial teaching methods. He encouraged children to learn from life's experiences rather than the orthodox daily lessons in the classroom. Prestolee school became known all over the north west as 'The do as you please school'. In the evening, the school was used as a Community Centre, catering for up to four hundred young people and known as the 'Palace of Youth' where dances and various cultural activities took place.

The playground which was constructed by the children themselves, contained a windmill, water gardens, fountains and a large paddling pool. During the 1930's, under O'Neil's headship, Prestolee school gained national recognition and attracted visitors from many parts of the north west to observe his 'Child Centred' method of teaching.

In the 1940's, O'Neil became heavily involved in the local community and helped organize the 'Festival of Prestolee' attracting thousands of visitors. Teddy O'Neil was still practicing his 'Essence of Teaching' methods of educating another generation of local children in 1946.

The canal flowing to the north of Prestolee and the Irwell flows south towards Stoneclough, passing Fletchers Paper Mill, the leading employer in the area. Robert Fletcher & Sons was founded in the early 1800's as paper bleachers. Fletcher was a man of vision and was soon manufacturing specialized paper products including waxed paper and in the early 1900's became one of Europe's largest manufacturers of cigarette papers. In 1921, Fletcher purchased a second mill at Greenfield, Oldham.

Figure 54 Ringley Locks

Having flowed past Prestolee the canal continues through Ringley Lock, after which the Irwell and the canal flow side by side to Ringley with it's ancient 'Pack Bridge' across the Irwell joining Ringley with 'Stoneclough'. Ringley was described by the late Derek Billington, in his book 'Affetside to Yarrow'. He writes:- *'Ringley was a hamlet in the township of Pilkington and no doubt sprang up around the ancient bridge spanning the Irwell which is mentioned as far back as the fifteenth century when William Wallwork had land there'.* In the 18th century it is spoken of as 'Ringley Fold' which usually denotes that the occupation of hand loom weaving was carried out. The Wallwork family were involved in the areas early textile business and Nathan Wallwork was a prosperous man much interested in religion. He was responsible for the re-building of St. Saviours Church and separate tower built in 1625 which still remain as do the Old Stocks. The bridge is mentioned in the 'Township Book of Halliwell' as a bridge that the folk of Halliwell had to share in keeping in repair. This was because it was a 'Hundred Bridge' and all taxpayers in 'The Hundred of Salford' were responsible for it's upkeep. The name 'Ringley' almost certainly comes from the old English word 'Hring' meaning circle and 'Ley' from the fact that it was a clearing. The banks of the Irwell at this point, in centuries past were heavily clad with trees and this must have been a clearing in a much larger 'Ringley Wood' that existed then, a small area of 'Ringley Wood' still exists nearby.

Figure 55 Ringley Bridge

As I enter Ringley with the Irwell to my right and the canal to the left alongside which stands the 'Horseshoe Inn', which was first licensed as a Pub in 1761. It was a scheduled stopping point for all Manchester bound packet boats on the canal which ran by the side of the 'Inn'. Parcels were left here for local deliveries and the landlord gladly served ale and food to the passengers before they continued their journey.

The 'Horseshoe' was also the location of a tradition going back to the middle ages. A ceremony took place here on the first Sunday in May, on the day after the anniversary sermons were preached at St. Saviours Church, with it's separate tower standing on land adjoining the 'Horseshoe'. During what became known as 'Ringley Wakes'. The ceremony was the election of the 'Mock Mayor of Ringley'. On the appointed day the customers of the 'Horseshoe' who were mainly miners from nearby collieries, would elect as 'Lord Mayor', the man who could drink the most ale. He was then formerly proclaimed in a speech by a man, styling himself for the occasion as the 'Lord Mayor's Clerk' which drew attention to the origin of the custom. It began here at Ringley in the early 1800's detailing the privileges of the Lord Mayor and also stressed his obligations, such as being lenient with anyone found drunk in any of the local Pubs. The Mayor then read out details of the sports and other activities taking place on the day and the prizes that could be won. He was then carried, shoulder high, by his followers, on a wooden chair wearing a military style braided jacket and a 'Shako' hat with a piece of bread on the end of a toasting fork as a symbol of his office. The party then toured anything up to nineteen Pubs in the area from Ringley to Stoneclough Brow, accompanied by a band and up to one hundred noisy followers finishing at the Ringley canal bridge. Here the Mayor read his speech again, by which time, more often than not, he was so drunk he could hardly speak and had probably fallen off his chair several times and put back on again by his followers. It was obvious by now that this was a job for a man who could 'hold his drink'. Finally the Mayor in all his splendour, was tipped into the canal and left floundering in the water for a few minutes, by which time he had probably sobered up. There was a more serious side to the ceremony, custom had it that the 'Lord Mayor of Ringley' was entitled to a pint of beer, a pipe of tobacco and a match in each of the three Pubs in the village, the 'Crown', the 'Lord Nelson' and the 'Horseshoe' every Sunday for the rest of the year, but only on condition that he turned up in his best clothes and definitely sober having first been to St. Saviour's Church, and according to custom the vicar couldn't refuse him entry.

Figure 56 Lord Mayor of Ringley

With the demise of the mining industry in the area the custom gradually died out and the last 'Lord Mayor of Ringley', a local man, Billy Pilkington, was inaugurated in the mid 1930's.

This whole area, bordering the canal and the Irwell has a long history of coalmining and generations of 'Ringleyites', as they became known had been employed in the nearby collieries, including Ringley, Outwood, Ladyshore and further down the Irwell, Wet Earth. Life in this picturesque part of rural

Lancashire had remained virtually unchanged for nearly two hundred years until, in the mid 1920's word spread that a Power Station was to be built by the Irwell, just down river from here at Ringley. After some controversy regarding it's size and location, construction of the station commenced in 1927 just south of Ringley Bridge. The main building, the 'Turbine Hall' containing five steam turbines was built on the Stoneclough side of the Irwell above Kearsley Green. Five cooling towers, each standing over 200 ft. high were built, three on the Ringley side of the river and another two beside the 'Turbine Hall' at Stoneclough. The two sites were connected by a steel service bridge spanning the Irwell. This is 'Kearsley Power Station' which now totally dominates this once rural community and after the original controversy surrounding the station and it's visual impact on the area, most local people were consoled by the fact the station created jobs for a number of 'Ringleyites'.

Figure 57 Kearsley Power Station

From the Power Station the matchstick, which has now travelled approximately fourteen miles from the start of it's journey, is approaching 'Giants Seat' where the canal again converges from the left, creating a narrow strip of land between the Irwell and the canal. This is 'Giants Seat Nursery' where I met Jim Kidd an apprentice gardener, who as we sat together, overlooking the river, told me the history of this fascinating strip of land. In the early 1900's standing beside the canal was a house, owned by 'Margaret Barlow' and over a number of years Margaret had created probably the most colourful garden in the area which gradually caught the attention of people passing in boats on the canal. Eventually the boats were mooring nearby and the passengers were asking Margaret if they could look round her lovely, colourful garden. She soon realized the potential of her garden and started to serve tea and her homemade cakes to the ever increasing number of visitors. After a couple of years Margaret had a Tea Room built and realizing that many children were among the visitors, attractions for the children were built including swings, a sand pit and a roundabout. By 1930 the garden had become so popular it became known as 'Margaret Barlow's Garden' and continued to thrive until 1939, when the canal breached between Giants Seat and Clifton leaving this stretch of the canal dry. Sadly the attraction of Margaret's garden ended and it was later sold to Levi Lansdale who has now developed the land into a plant nursery.

Most of the mines in this area were sunk in the mid to late 1700's along the 'Pendleton Fault', the line of which the Irwell follows as it flows towards Salford. Most early mines were subject to roof falls, which had proved fatal on a number of occasions. These mines along the 'Fault', as had been the case at Ladyshore in 1835 were liable to severe flooding. They were extremely dangerous places to work, to depths of two hundred feet below ground. The conditions were difficult for the miners, but in the early 1800's few people realized just how many women and children were being exploited underground. Some miners employed their own children, so the child's wages were kept in the family.

Whole families, husband, wife and children worked together, some of the children could be as young as seven years old. The first job given to these youngsters was working underground as a 'Trapper', which entailed working the trap door that ventilated the shaft and allowed coal wagons through. The children just sat by the trap door in total darkness for twelve hours a day just opening and shutting the door. It is said that 'Sarah', an eight year old, told her friend **"I'm a Trapper', I have to work in the dark and I'm scared".**

After being dug or blasted from the seam, the coal was transported in wooden sleds pulled mainly by women or young boys, these were called 'Drawers' or 'Putters'. If the tub was too heavy for one 'Drawer' another child called a 'Thrutcher' was called upon to help. Some of these children were almost bald, their hair having been rubbed off by pushing their heads against the tubs. The only light the 'Drawers' had was a candle stuck to their head with a piece of wet clay. 'Drawers' often pushed their tubs along miles of tunnels in a working day and were constantly threatened by 'Roof Falls'.

On the 26th July, 1849, it was reported in the 'Bolton Chronicle' that:- *'William Longworth, aged twelve years, son of William Longworth, a collier. The boy who was employed as a 'Drawer' at the coalpit of Messrs. Scowcroft and Longworth, near Doffcocker, was killed instantly when a stone weighing in excess of one ton fell on him. His friend, James Williams was also thrown down by the stone and severely injured'.*

Just days later on August 4th, 1849, it was again reported:- *'A Coal Pit Accident'. 'On Wednesday evening last, about six o'clock, Andrew Harwood, aged ten years, the son of Andrew Harwood, died from injuries sustained from the fall of a stone, when at work at the Coalpit belonging to Messrs. Scowcroft and*

Longworth. Another boy, William Croston, was close by and narrowly escaped injury'.

Women were exploited and abused in the mines. They were used as cheap labour and were described for wage purposes as 'One half of a man'. Women miners dressed as men to escape violence and sexual abuse. These women, because of their working conditions, became violent and abusive to others. They were regularly heard bickering among themselves using language that some of their male colleagues seldom used.

Most of these women had not gone down the Pits by choice. Often circumstances forced them to. There are many sad stories relating to these unfortunate women miners. This is Peggy Lowe's story:-'*In 1828, Peggy's husband Jack worked as a face worker at 'Ringley Pit'. Sadly Jack fell down the shaft and was killed instantly. Peggy was devastated. However, the mine owners offered her Jack's job so she could feed her family. Peggy accepted and became a Miner'.*

Betty Harris from Little Bolton became a 'Drawer' when she was twenty three and told a friend:- ' **If she didn't work hard enough for twelve hours a day, her husband would beat her'.**

There are many such stories highlighting the conditions under which the women and children worked until reforms in the mines were introduced in the mid 1800's.

As Jim and I sat looking down on the Irwell flowing beneath us, he continued to tell me the history of 'Giants Seat' and the area surrounding the river. On the south side of the Irwell, opposite us and on higher ground is Fletchers canal which was built to feed water to 'Wet Earth' Colliery, just a mile down river from 'Giants Seat'. Sunk around 1730, this mine was one of the earliest recorded deep mines along the Irwell valley. The site was originally owned by the 'Edensor' and 'Heathcote' families, who engaged a local engineer, Matthew Fletcher to dig the first deep shafts to the coal seams. This became known as the 'Gal Pit' after the 'Galloway Ponies', the 'Wet Earth' working horses which were the original colliery 'Horse Power'. The ponies did their shift at the Pit Head, walking steadily round a twenty foot circle, operating the 'Horse Engine', a hoist which lifted and lowered men and coal to and from the galleries deep underground.

The mine soon began to flood, hence it's name 'Wet Earth' Colliery. James Brindley who had gained a reputation for solving problems relating to water engineering and gained the nickname 'The Schemer'. He devised a pumping system which pumped water through a tunnel at Giants Seat and into the canal known as 'Th'owd Cut', and as Jim said **'That feller made water go uphill'.**

Special boats were built to use the new canal, known as 'Skeleton Boats'. These were much narrower than the standard coal boats and were described, at the time as 'looking like floating skeletons'. These boats transferred the coal from the mine to coal barges for delivery to Salford and Manchester.

In 1791 this section of the Manchester, Bolton and Bury canal was built, known locally as 't' New Cut'. Fletchers canal joined the waterway where the new canal crossed over the Irwell via. the Clifton Aqueduct.

As we travel south east we pass, to our left, 'Clifton House', commissioned by Matthew Fletcher and completed in 1763. Fletcher lived there, with his family until his death in 1808. The house remained in the Fletcher family until the 1850's.

In the early 1860's, the Pilkington family took over the colliery and moved into the house. This was before they established the famous Pottery and Tile Company nearby. In the late 1800's, Clifton House employed a particularly strict gamekeeper who used to make children who were caught 'scrumping' apples on the estate, weed the pathway up to the house with a kitchen fork. During World War Two this section of the Irwell valley, including 'Kearsley Power Station' and the nearby 'Chloride Battery Factory' were prime targets for German bombers. The valley was protected by anti aircraft batteries and barrage balloons. Kearsley Power Station was identified as a potential German target. One of the area's most famous visitors was Lawrence Stephen Lowry, probably Lancashire's most famous artist. Although he spent most of his later years in Cheshire, he spent many weeks in the Irwell valley, painting and drawing 'Ramsford Bridge' which spanned 'Fletchers Canal', close to 'Pilkington's Tile Factory' and in 1920 he depicted 'Wet Earth Colliery' on canvas. 'Wet Earth' prospered for over 170 years until it's closure in 1928. At this point the Irwell has travelled approximately twenty miles from it's source high above Bacup. From here it will flow a further thirty eight miles joining the Manchester Ship Canal, the Mersey and out to the Irish Sea.

Figure 58 Wet Earth Colliery by L.S. Lowry

An unknown 18th century poet wrote of the upper valleys of the river. He writes:-

> *'Behold, behold, the wondrous eyes*
> *The towering hills that reach the skies*
> *The fertile plain and vale below*
> *Where the lovely streams and Irwell flow'*

It is said that before the Romans arrived here around the time of Christ, Celtic tribes farmed the lush uplands bordering the river. When they did arrive they were so impressed with the idyllic landscape and the beauty of the river, the Centurians built their villas along it's banks. From the early eighteen hundreds as the industrial revolution enveloped most of Lancashire, the Irwell gradually then rapidly, became more and more polluted, as ever increasing numbers of factories, mills and chemical works were built along it's banks. The Irwell has been described as 'An angry river fed by so many angry brooks and streams'. In 1902 it was recorded that four hundred and forty five firms were polluting the river everyday. In the 18th century people living as far south as central Manchester could walk down to the Irwell with buckets to fill with water from the river for domestic use. But just seventy years later in 1869, about the time the Suez Canal was built, the Irwell got the nickname 'The Sewage Canal'.

The river is now heading towards Agecroft with it's colliery and power station, passing under Clifton aqueduct carrying the canal, flowing from our left, over the river, adjacent to the enormous 'Pilkington' Tile and Pottery Works. A short distance further the skyline is dominated by the 'Agecroft Power Station', built on the site of 'Agecroft Hall'. The building dated back to medieval times, owned originally by Richard de Langley and his descendants. The Hall was originally surrounded by a moat, which later became an ornamental pond.

Around 1820, the building was threatened with demolition when it was proposed to build a railway line from Manchester to Bolton, passing right through the Hall. But with the intervention of Mr. Buck, a local businessman who campaigned to save the Hall and offered £5,000. to the Railway Company to divert the line, which they eventually did and the Hall was saved. However one hundred years later, the Hall became derelict and was again threatened with demolition. But in 1925 it was saved this time by an American, Thomas C. Williams Junior of Richmond, U.S.A. who had arrived in the area looking to fulfil his dream of creating an English Country Mansion in his home state. Williams was determined to save the Hall, which he bought and had it carefully dismantled stone by stone and panel by panel including the minstrels gallery. Every beam and stone was carefully numbered, crated and shipped across the Atlantic to 'Richmond', Virginia, where it stands overlooking the 'James River' surrounded by landscaped gardens and maintained by the 'Agecroft Association'. Just down river from Agecroft Bridge stands 'Kersal Cell', an imposing timber framed Manor House built in 1563, when it was occupied by a group (or a Cell) of the 'Reformed Benedictine Monks Cluny'. Hence the name 'Cell'. It is the second oldest building in Salford.

In the early 1700's, 'Kersal Cell' was the home of John Byrom and his family. Byrom was a man of many talents. He was a prolific writer, penning numerous poems and letters. He also wrote a number of hymns, the most famous of which was 'Christians Awake'. Byrom was a gifted linguist, he was fluent in Latin, French and Italian. It is said that he got his inspiration from strolling through the wooded clough of the Irwell valley, rowing leisurely along the river or sitting by a grove of yew trees standing between his house and the Irwell, bearing in mind this was many years before the industrial revolution blighted the Irwell. Byrom spent a year in France, giving him the opportunity to improve his French. On his return to 'Kersal' he perfected a system of 'shorthand' which was the forerunner of all later variations of shorthand. He settled down again to his quiet rural life by the Irwell and his beloved 'Kersal Cell', where he died in 1763.

Figure 59 Kersal Cell

Barely half a mile south of here. Sunday, July 30th, 1944, was just another lovely summer's day for George Morris, a forty five year old 'Air Raid Warden'. This was the highlight of his week, spending a few hours 'pottering' around his allotment adjoining the 'Littleton Road playing fields' by the Irwell at Pendlebury. Normally, at this time, his wife Caroline brought him his afternoon flask of tea, as Caroline opened the gate to the allotment, with her usual **"It's me love"** they both heard the sound of a low flying aircraft approaching from the west.

Caroline remembered George asked her to fetch some scissors from their house nearby to cut some roses. She collected the scissors and on her way back to the allotment she saw a large aircraft flying low, overhead and recalls **"I thought it was doing stunts"**. At that moment George realized that the plane was in serious trouble and shouted **"run for it Carrie"**. She goes on to say **"I ran behind an air raid shelter, there was a loud explosion. I ran home to see if the children were safe and then ran back to George's 'Plot' where I found him lying on the ground.** He said **"Carrie, my left leg has gone"**.

George seemed to be doing well in hospital, but died a few hours later. The cause of death was a 'Pulmonary Embolism' brought on by the fracture to his leg.

Another fatality on the ground was Mrs Lucy Bamford, who was at home in nearby Langley Road. She also appeared to be recovering from her 'blast' injuries', was discharged from hospital but died at her son's home on August 11th. The aircraft in question was a 'Lancaster' bomber, number P.B. 304 of 106 Squadron, based at R.A.F. Metheringham, Lincolnshire. The pilot, Flight Lieutenant Peter Lines, although early in his flying career, was considered to be an exceptionally good young pilot. The brand new 'Lancaster' had been on a bombing raid on German positions at 'Cahagned' in Normandy, in support of British troops on the ground. The attacking force comprised four hundred and sixty two 'Lancasters', two hundred 'Halifaxes' and thirty 'Mosquitoes'. But due to cloud cover the target area, was not visible. The Lancasters were ordered to descend through the cloud cover to bomb at low level.

However, the crews found that this was not possible and were eventually ordered to return to base, still carrying their bombs, which they could not ditch over the 'English Channel', due to all the allied shipping supplying the British invading forces. For whatever reason this 'Lancaster' was forced to fly north over Yorkshire, possibly having been hit by German 'flak' as it circled over Normandy. The aircraft was in trouble as it descended over Manchester, low on fuel, attempting to get to it's base in Lincolnshire. Many witness accounts describe the 'Lancaster' flying low, with port engine trouble, attempting to land on the 'Littleton Road playing fields', bordering the Irwell. The first attempt was aborted and a second attempt was made by Flight Lieutenant Lines. He nearly made it, but a wing clipped the rooftops of houses in 'Regatta Street' and the 'Lancaster' crashed on the bank of the 'Irwell'.

There was a pause after the crash before the bombs on board exploded, killing the crew of seven and as a result of the explosion, George Morris and Lucy Bamford died from their injuries. It is said that up to eighty local people were also injured.

Two weeks later the following appeal appeared in the 'Salford City Reporter' :-

AN APPEAL

By his Worship the Mayor of Salford, Alderman Leonard Webb. J.P. on behalf of the R.A.F. Benevolent Fund.

The following is written in tribute to the gallant crew of an aircraft which recently developed serious trouble whilst passing over the City, but by superb skill was crash landed on open ground adjoining the City, thus avoiding a tremendous loss of life. All the crew died, the tribute says :-

He circled here, he circled there,
this pilot high up in the air
looking for somewhere, but in vain
to land his almost done plane.

His thoughts were for his gallant men
who had been on 'Ops' and back again
with a fully laden bomber craft
'T' was enough to send this pilot 'daft'
when he thought of the houses down below
he was doing his best to miss them though
He tried to reach a playing field
with nothing to help him to act as a shield.

So praying to god, he made a bold bid
no hero's done better than this man did
but something appeared to hit a wing
and sent him reeling with a swing
into the side of a darned old tip

which he might have cleared with an extra flip.

But it wasn't to be and this man died
along with his gallant crew beside
let us remember as long as we live
these men, for us, their lives did give
there was only two died among us all
God needed them both, so gave them a call
so they could give thanks to the pilot and crew
from the people below over whom they flew.

By: J. BELSHAW OF PENDLETON

At nearby Agecroft Cemetery is a memorial stone remembering those seven men who died on that summer's day in 1944. They are named as Flight Lieutenant Peter Lines from Purley, Sussex, Sergeant Arthur Young, an Afro Caribbean from Cardiff, Sergeant Mohand Singh from Punjab, Sergeant Raymond Barnes a local man, Sergeant John Bruce Thornley Davenport from Market Drayton, Flying Officer John Steele of Bradford, Flying Officer Harry Reid from Toronto, Canada. They are all remembered at their Home Base, Metheringham, Lincolnshire.

At this point I refer to Cyril Bracegirdle's fascinating book 'The Dark River' in which he writes :-

'Now we are nearing the great conurbation itself, habitation of about two million people, who are here in houses, offices, factories and power stations because, aeons ago a spring began to gush forth on the 'Vale of the Deer above Bacup'. Bracegirdle

goes on to describe many events and stories of people and places along the Irwell.

Over the centuries the river has flooded on a number of occasions. For the Irwell to flood over it's banks in the 19th century was a rare event. Many dams and weirs controlled it's course, taming and confining a river once wild and free. In former days the Irwell wreaked immense damage to the humans who dared to block it's way with bricks and concrete.

One of the worst and best documented was 'The Great Flood' of 1866, which struck on an otherwise calm November day. The rising waters had already caused the river Tonge in Bolton to rise dramatically, causing excessive flooding around Darcy Lever. Now the Irwell was to wreak havoc for miles, causing misery to many thousands of people living along it's banks and surrounding areas in the riverside slums of Salford and Manchester, who lived in cheap cellar rooms. These families stood no chance as the waters crashed through windows, swamping their homes in seconds. In most of the dwellings around Lower Broughton, water rose as high as the upper floors, where hundreds of families crowded together in the attics and upper rooms, praying that the water would rise no higher. People were seen clinging to anything that would float as the muddy, brown, stinking water carried them along with dead animals, trees, broken furniture, even a group of hens perched on an old hen coop was seen floating towards Broughton Lane. From the racecourse at 'The Cliff', all the way to the 'Crescent' at Salford, the Irwell had become a moving lake. The wooden, tubular roofed bridge which led to 'Castle

Irwell', watched by hundreds of people, was ripped from it's supports and carried, in one piece as far as the 'Crescent' where it came to rest. From Agecroft to Kersal Dale, round the racecourse curve, to the 'Bluff' at Broughton and beyond was a torrent of putrid water. The aftermath of the disaster was reported at length in the 'Free Lance' a satirical magazine of the time. they wrote :-

'Last week, every brook became a river, every rill, a torrent. Every pond a whirlpool. Cellars   flooded. Works inundated, machinery ruined, thereby putting many people out of work. The damage done to the pretty borders in 'Peel Park' was horrific. The lovely promenade had been covered in mud and debris, where a number of departed cats and dogs were found among the dahlia and aster beds. The Palatine Bridge was, at one time, under four feet of water and in the Strangeways area many families were marooned in their homes and pleasure boats were brought from 'Belle Vue' to help in the rescue. Only one death was reported. That was in the Broughton district. A man lost his footing in Duke Street, was swept away and drowned.

Figure 60 the Great Flood

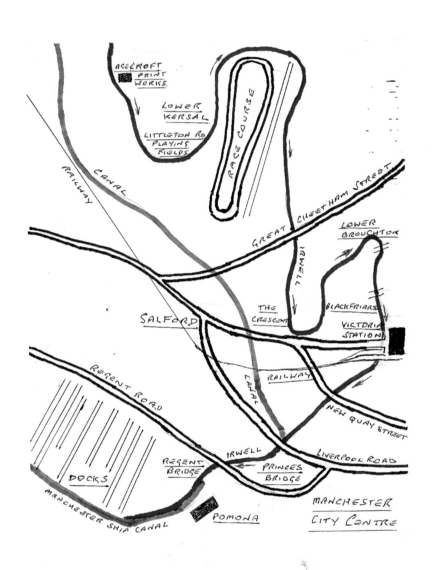

Map 11 River Irwell to Salford Docks

I first saw the Irwell in 1946, shortly after the 'Burnden Disaster'. Mam, dad, my sister and I went to visit my dad's younger sister 'Auntie Kathleen', who was a Franciscan Nun looking after orphan children at a convent 'Our Lady of Lourdes Home', in Didsbury, Manchester. We left Bolton on the green number eight, 'Salford City Transport' bus, heading for Salford. I had never travelled so far on a bus before. As we got on the bus, mam said **"let's go upstairs, you'll be able to see much more"**. As we travelled towards Manchester there was really nothing to see, just houses and fields. But after about half an hour I looked to my left, through the bus window and for a few seconds, I saw a big 'Horseshoe shaped river'. Having only lived in Bolton all of my eight years, the only river I had seen was the one at Barrow Bridge, nothing like the one to my left. Sometime later, I was told that what I had seen was the river Irwell flowing round the 'Salford Crescent'. The bus carried on to Salford where we got off and walked up the hill to 'Deansgate' where we were to catch the red, number one 'Manchester Corporation' bus to Gatley.

As we walked along Deansgate we were struck by the desolation around us. We were surrounded by the 'shells' of once impressive buildings. Dad who was obviously somewhat surprised at what we saw, was the first to speak and all he could say was **"it's the bombing Al"**. We had never experienced this in Bolton. A couple of years earlier, around 1944, I had walked with my Grandpa Peters, from Lower Pools, up Chorley Old Road to the 'Bob's Smithy' Pub. It was just going dark and as I stood with grandpa, looking south, across Manchester and Salford, I saw the sky light up on the horizon and searchlights piercing the darkness. There was no sound. I never forgot that sight and a few weeks later grandpa told me that what I had seen was the 'Two Cities' being bombed and what I was looking at as we walked along Deansgate, some two years later was probably the result of that bombing.

We boarded the number one Gatley bus to 'Our lady of Lourdes' Convent where we were greeted with warm hugs from Auntie Kathleen and her 'Sisters', who were safe and well.

A number of bridges across the Irwell have come and gone over the years. The first bridge was almost certainly a wooden structure close to the present 'Victoria Bridge', later to be replaced, in 1368, by a stone structure, it is said, at a cost of £30. Halfway across the bridge was a small chapel which, after many years was no longer used as a place of worship and the lower of it's two rooms became a prison. Many a drunk spent a sleepless night there, fighting off the ever hungry rats. The prisoners also faced possible drowning and it is recorded, that, at least one unfortunate individual drowned during a night of heavy rain, as the dungeon was just above the water level, and was likely to flood. The Chapel was finally demolished in 1775. An iron chain suspension bridge was built in 1826 to span the Irwell between Broughton and Pendleton. This was one of Europe's first suspension bridges.

On 12th of April, 1831, a detachment of seventy four men of the 60th Rifle Corps had carried out an exercise on Kersal Moor, under the command of Lieutenant Peter Slingsby Fitzgerald. As they returned to their Barracks in Salford, by way of the bridge,

the soldiers, who were marching in step, four abreast, felt the bridge begin to vibrate in time with their marching. Finding the vibration, as one said later, **"a pleasant sensation".** Some of them started whistling a marching tune. As they headed across the bridge, it began to vibrate even more, when there was a loud crack, one of the
bridge support columns collapsed into the Irwell, some twenty feet below, taking part of the bridge and the Rifle Corps with it. Fortunately, they all survived after a good soaking and some broken limbs.   After the incident there was some loss of confidence in suspension bridges. However, this did not stop the building of many more in the subsequent years. The main consequence of the collapse was that the British Army issued an order to 'break step' when soldiers were crossing a bridge. French soldiers were also ordered to 'break step' on bridges, as marching was cited as a contributory factor in the collapse of the 'Angers Bridge' in France, during a storm in 1850 killing over two hundred soldiers. The suspension bridge at Broughton was eventually replaced by a footbridge which was formally opened in April, 1924. In 1896, a new footbridge was built over the Irwell between Peel Park and Broughton, officially opened by the Mayor and members of the local Council, who, on the spur of the moment, did what they were warned not to do. That is 'have a dip in the Irwell'. The only comment from the local Press was :- **"We hope they liked it".**

By the 1750's, the 'Mersey and the Irwell Navigation Company' was operating a regular service along the Irwell between Manchester and Liverpool. The vessels used were occasionally pulled by horses, but more often by teams of three or four young men using tow ropes. However, the vessels carried a large square sail, which would be set in favourable winds, propelling the boat forward, so the men simply jumped on board to ride freely. In 1766, there were fourteen of these boats trading from Manchester and six from Salford, on the journey to Runcorn and Warrington, by two types of craft, the 'Packet Boats' and the faster 'Swift Packet Boats'. The 'Packet Boats' were a large spacious craft, about sixty feet long and built to carry large numbers of passengers, their luggage and some cargo. They were normally drawn by two horses at a leisurely pace. The 'Swift Boats' were more slender, built for speed and carried passengers only. They were drawn by up to three horses, ridden by red jacketed 'Jockeys'. The leader carried a horn which he used to warn people on the towpath to give way. These specially trained horses were the 'Elite' of river transport and could match the speed of the 'mail coaches' on the roads. On May Day the 'Swift Horses' would be 'decked out' in their polished harnesses and brasses by their proud 'Jockeys'. These river expresses had no timetable, they ran at any time, day or night to catch the 'Mersey tides'.

One hundred years later in the mid 1800's, Steam Packet boats were a common sight along the Irwell and Mersey from Manchester and Salford. In 1866, a correspondent for the 'Manchester City News' reported on a 'Pleasure Trip' on one of the Steam Packet Boats, from Salford. He writes:-

'It was a great treat to my sister and me when my mother took us, occasionally, on a fine summer's afternoon for a sail on the river. We descended from Blackfriars Bridge by some stone

steps where the boat was waiting below. We took our seats, the boat started and we were soon gliding past the backs of old houses and mills. Gradually the scenery on either side became less industrial and instead of grimy buildings there appeared green grassy banks, trees and cottages with gardens before them full of flowers. By this time the water was purer and the air cleaner. On we went, past green fields where cows were feeding or lying lazily in the shade. Farmhouses were dotted here and there, ducks and geese swam near the banks. Occasionally we saw a man fishing with rod and line. There were stopping places on the way where passengers could alight by a sort of platform which jutted out into the river. You could leave at Barton, Patricroft or Eccles. We were to leave near Barton and go up a country lane till we found a farmhouse or cottage, where we had tea. After this we strolled about gathering wild flowers to take home, till the return of the boat about six or seven o'clock'.

There were two packet boats named the 'Punch' and the 'Judy'.

Figure 61 Blackfriars Bridge

Sailing peacefully through a rural landscape like the one described, wasn't the only reason that local people loved the 'Boat Trips'. These cost one penny from Victoria Bridge to the main attraction on the Irwell, that was 'Pamona Gardens', originally known as the 'Strawberry Gardens', which was an 'Oasis' of Botanical Gardens mixed with a Zoo and pleasure attractions. The centrepiece was the elegant 'Pamona Palace', with a clock tower over fifty feet high lit by gas after dark. The gardens covered an area of over twenty acres from the Irwell to Chester Road. Weather permitting, there were military bands and street dancers. Whit weekend was non-stop entertainment, including a great carnival, ballet performances and the star attraction was 'Blondin' the famous tightrope walker who performed on a wire stretched high above the open air dance floor. There were rowing regattas along the river. In 1874, the T.U.C. celebrated it's tenth anniversary at the gardens by holding a gathering of an estimated eighty thousand people. In September, 1842, the first Manchester and Salford Regatta was rowed on the stretch of the Irwell from 'Throstle Nest' to Regent Road bridge.

The Manchester Guardian recorded that :-

'There was sunshine and a pleasant breeze, with many flags flying. The river banks were crowded with thousands of spectators. The favoured ones in the enclosure being entertained by the 'Salford Borough Band'. The occasion was, in every way, worthy of the town and the improved state of the river'.

This improvement was not to last. The Regattas were abandoned in 1863.

"Had the 'Irwell' won again"?

By 1887, the once iconic 'Pamona Gardens' were surrounded by chimneys, belching out smoke adding to the endless smog that hung over the Irwell and in that year a nearby chemical factory exploded, badly damaging the 'Pamona Palace' beyond repair and adding further pollution to the river. But this poisoning of the whole area did not destroy the rare plant life that, remarkably still thrives in this 'Irwell Oasis'. **Had the Irwell won**

again? Not quite. The 'Matchstick' is now approaching 'Blackfriars' and it's bridge. This area and the next mile are the source of a number of events and characters over many years. One such character was 'Mark Addy', probably Salford's most famous 'Irwellian'. Mark was born in a tenement block near 'Blackfriars Bridge' known as the 'Stage Buildings' in 1838. His father, also called Mark was a 'Boatman' who owned a number of craft for hire on the 'Irwell'. Young Mark grew up by the river, helping his dad as 'crew' on the boats and was totally unaware of the swirling 'sewage canal' on which he spent most of his young life. Around 1852, Mark learned to swim at 'Greengate Baths'. During that year he had already saved his best friend from drowning twice, in the Irwell. The second time by floating out to his friend on a plank of wood and 'towing' him to safety.

Some years later Mark married and acquired a Tavern on the Salford side of the river. Whenever anyone was in difficulties in the 'Irwell', the cry went out 'bring Mark Addy', who would immediately abandon his customers and race to the river.

On one occasion Addy was returning from a funeral in a new black suit with a valuable gold watch in his pocket, when the cry went up *'a child is in the river!'.* Mark rushed to the spot and *'without divesting himself of a single garment'* plunged in and rescued the child. As he stood dripping, before the crowd of excited onlookers, one said **"Mark th'as spoilt thi' clothes"**. **"What of that"** came the answer. **"I reckon it will also have made a mess of mi watch, but it doesn't matter, there was a life at stake"**.

Figure 62 Mark Addy

In the early 1870's a drunken and mentally unstable woman threw herself in the river in an attempted suicide. Mark again raced to the rescue, but due to her struggles to fight him off, Mark was almost drowned himself, but despite the cry's of onlookers to leave her and save himself he subdued her and brought her ashore. Another life saved.

At a later date Addy was roused from his sleep by a boatman who informed him that a woman was drowning in the river. Rushing out in his night-clothes, he rowed out to the woman but was unable to get her into the boat as she weighed over 17 stone so, holding her head out of the water with one hand and rowing the boat with the other he managed to float her to the bank. During his relatively short life, Mark Addy snatched no fewer than fifty five souls from a watery, poisonous death. Mark won numerous awards and medals for his bravery, including the gold medal of the 'Salford Humane Society'. In November, 1878, Addy received the following letter from the Prime Minister, Benjamin Disraeli and quotes:-

' Sir. The attention of the Sovereign having been called to the repeated acts of heroism performed by you in saving, at the risk of your own life, those of many of her Majesty's subjects from drowning in the river Irwell. I have the gratification to inform you that the Queen has been graciously pleased to confer on you, in recognition of your gallantry and daring, the honour and distinction of the Albert Medal of the first class. I have accordingly instructed the Secretary of State to take the necessary steps to give effect to her Majesty's commands'.

I have the honour to be your obedient servant, - Disraeli.

Mark Addy continued to save lives for another eleven years until Whit Monday in 1889, when he was called to save a young boy in difficulties at Factory Lane as he had done so many times before. After struggling with the panic stricken lad, during which Mark had swallowed a lethal cocktail of chemicals which made up the waters of the 'Irwell', he finally saved the lad. But just days later, Mark, already suffering ill health was taken ill and died aged fifty one. Mark Addy beat the Irwell fifty five times, but the Irwell waited until that fateful day 'Whit Monday', when it took Mark Addy, a true 'Irwellian'.

In 1785, the 'New Bailey Bridge' was built across the Irwell connecting Salford with Manchester in the Chapel Street area.

It was December, 1813 and the whole country was experiencing the most severe winter in living memory. Fairs were being held on the frozen 'River Thames'. The ice of the Irwell was not thick enough to hold a Fair, but a winter fog hung over the Irwell valley for days.

Lavinia Robinson, an attractive thirty year old single schoolmistress, whose family were surprised that at thirty years old she had not married. After one failed relationship, she met and became engaged to John, a handsome young surgeon. However, a few days previously the couple had quarrelled outside Lavinia's house in Bridge Street, witnessed by her neighbours, who said, **"John strode off shouting, it's all over Lavinia"**.

On the night of December, 13th, Lavinia told her father she was going out to meet John on the nearby, recently constructed 'New Bailey Bridge' to 'patch things up'. Her father tried to convince her not to go out alone on such a bitterly cold, foggy night. But Lavinia, a strong willed young woman ignored her father's pleas and left the house into the darkness.

It is said that she did meet John on the bridge and tried to convince him to continue their relationship, but John rejected her, pushed her aside and left her standing on the bridge. She was never seen alive again.

Days later it was suggested the river be dragged, but the weather had become even colder and the ice so thick, that idea was out of the question.

Some weeks later, on the morning of February, 17th, 1814, a Mr Goodier was walking by the Irwell, when he saw Lavinia floating by, encased in a block of ice with her head protruding from one end of the block. After her perfectly preserved body was recovered from the Irwell, Mr. Goodier, is reported to have said **"she floated by like the Irwell's Ophelia".**

The local newspaper of the day described Lavinia as:-

'This ill scarred maiden, reclining on a sandbank, environed by masses of ice, with icicles gemming her hair in place of orange blossoms. Decay had hardly touched her loveliness with his effacing finger'.

Many hundreds attended the funeral of the 'Manchester Ophelia'. When Lavinia was laid to rest in St. John's Churchyard, the following inscription was carved on her gravestone :-

More lasting than in lines of art
Thy spoiled character impress
Thy worth engraved in every heart
Thy loss bewailed in every breast

About twenty years later, again in the 'New Bailey Bridge' area, one of the most interesting and amusing characters ever to grace the annuls of the Irwell caught the attention of people living in this part of Salford. His name was Sam Scott, an American who's background is a complete mystery. In the newspapers of the time there are occasional references of Sam's obsession with jumping from great heights into comparatively shallow water. He became known locally as 'Sam the Jumper', who attracted attention and some money by spectacular leaps into the Irwell which, in the 1830's, was still relatively unpolluted. In December, 1837, word spread throughout the area that the 'Jumper' would perform his most daring feat, leaping from the top of a five story warehouse overlooking 'New Bailey Bridge'. At the appointed time, a huge crowd gathered by the Irwell as Sam appeared on the warehouse roof wearing 'Lace Drawers', a red flannel shirt and a 'Bladder' stretched over his head, probably thinking this would give him some protection if he landed 'head first'. He waved to the crowd and leapt into the river.

A local newspaper reported the event, quoting :-

'He presented an erect position during the time he was in the air, with arms and legs 'spread eagled' until he hit the water, causing a large wave along the Irwell'.

A couple of minutes passed, people were thinking the worst, would Sam ever re-surface? Whereupon a head, complete with bladder appeared. The 'Jumper' had survived, even though the Irwell, at that point, was no more than twelve feet deep. After further exploits in and around the Irwell, the novelty of the 'Jumper' lost it's popularity and Sam Scott mysteriously disappeared. However, it was rumoured, at the time he was 'accidentally' hanged on Waterloo Bridge, London, in January, 1841.

In 1844, the new 'Albert Bridge' was built to replace the 'New Bailey Bridge' and the first vehicle to cross the 'Albert Bridge', was a 'donkey and cart'.

The opening ceremony was held with dignitaries from both towns crossing the bridge from each side and meeting in the middle accompanied by military bands. There were formal handshakes before they sat down to refreshments laid on special tables overlooking the river. In 1846, close to 'Victoria Bridge', two young engineers, William and Colin Mather bought an old Ironworks near Chapel Street, Salford. This partnership became, in the 20th century, 'Mather & Platt Ltd'. Their first major project was the construction of an early steam ship which was sailed down the Irwell, along the Mersey to Liverpool and across to the 'Isle of Man'. Most seasoned engineers of the day were convinced that it would sink as soon as it left the Mersey estuary. Those two young men proved the 'experts' wrong. Their Company later moved from the Irwell to what was to become 'Trafford Park', where they produced a revolutionary new method of putting out fires, the 'Sprinkler System'.

We are now approaching Manchester City Centre and 'Regent Bridge'. It was just about here in February, 1828, that the biggest cargo vessel ever built on the Irwell, the 'Emma' was to be launched. This was a big occasion, with about three hundred invited guests celebrating on the deck. As the launch time approached, the band of the 'Ninth Regiment' burst forth into a variety of military marches accompanied by cannon fire. At the appointed time, as the gathered crowds cheered, spurred on by a roll of drums, the 'Emma' glided into the Irwell and crashed into the Salford Bank, throwing the 'Dignitaries' into the polluted river, causing absolute panic. Despite the efforts of a number of rescuers people were drowning. On that fateful day thirty eight of Salford and Manchester's most respected citizens perished in the Irwell. It was later reported that some of the victims died, not by drowning, but by poisoning after swallowing the polluted water.

From Regent Road the river flows south west to Woden Street footbridge and Pomona Docks.

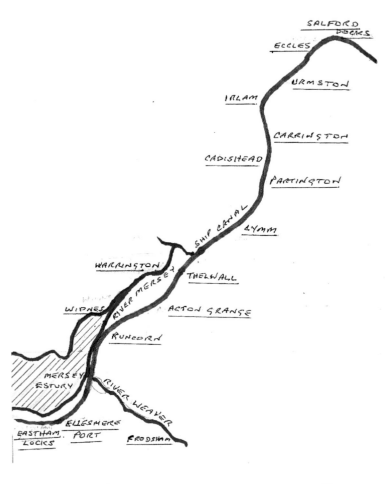

ROUTE OF MANCHESTER SHIP CANAL

Map 12 Manchester Ship Canal to the River Mersey

In the early 1800's plans were discussed by the most innovative Victorian Civil Engineers to build a canal from the Pomona area to the Mersey estuary, giving the cities of Manchester, Salford and the heavily industrialized towns of rural Lancashire access to the Irish Sea and beyond. After discussions at the highest level and a detailed survey of the proposed route, Royal Assent was given in 1885 to build the proposed waterway. When completed the canal would be approximately thirty six miles long, passing through the Lancashire and Cheshire plain, finally discharging into the Mersey estuary at Eastham. In November, 1887, work began at various locations along the route and in that year, a new word appeared in the English language, that word is 'canalized'. From 'Pomona', the Irwell was incorporated into the newly constructed 'Manchester Ship Canal' in effect 'canalizing' the river.

This was literally the end of the Irwell as Mancunians had known it for centuries.

In the late 19th century, Joseph Anthony wrote this poem :-

Who'er hath seen dark Irwell's tide
It's sombre look and sullen guide
Would never deem that it, I ween
Had never brighter, gayer been
When Irwell rolled by feudal tower
By shady grove and fairy bower
When on her banks so oft was born
Sweet music of the hunters horn
Forests are here, but none of trees
Forests are here, the homes of men
Mancunians sons are as the leaves
Which bloomed upon the forest then

Flow sweetly Irwell as you did before the machines came.

Only the first half mile of the canal is actually in Manchester. Leaving 'Pomona' it heads west into Salford, flowing past the thriving Manchester Docks and Quays, arriving at 'Trafford Park' then south west, passing Daveyhulme and Flixton.

The matchstick should now have a smooth, uninterrupted journey along the canal to it's ultimate destination, passing Irlam and Cadishead.

The history of the construction and later development of the canal is well documented in various publications, describing the logistics and construction of the canal along with the human stories associated with it.

The operative word associated with the construction of the canal was 'manpower' and the men who provided the power were the hundreds of 'Navvy's', most of whom had arrived from Ireland. His task, ten hours a day, was to fill his 'barrow', more often than not, push it up a wooden ramp, empty it, return to be loaded and repeat the process day after day, a result of which these men were described as 'having arms down to their knees' and 'muscles in their spit'.

Figure 63 A Barrow run

Hundreds of local men were recruited at various points along the route of the canal. However, the main contractors needed skilled men in various trades including bricklayers, carpenters and machine operators, the majority of which were recruited from all over the north west.   All these men, some with families, needed accommodation along with shops and other services. It was decided that a number of temporary settlements of pre-fabricated buildings would be constructed at various locations along the canal. The largest was at 'Acton Grange', Daresbury, near Warrington.

These buildings were of a good standard and compared favourably with the average working man's home in many north west towns.

With relatively high wages and bonuses the settlements became the north west 'Klondyke' of the 1890's. These men worked hard for up to ten hours a day, but they also liked to 'play hard'. Consequently these thriving communities attracted many 'hangers on' such as members of the 'oldest profession', some of whom, along the 'Mersey estuary' used old 'flat boats' as accommodation. These boats were put to various uses, some even became 'Floating Chapels', along with a number of 'Floating Clergymen'.

The canal continues to flow south west through Cheshire farmland between Cadishead and Partington, under the Warburton High Level Bridge, passing the picturesque little town of Lymm. Then skirting south of Glazebrook, passing through the centre of Warrington and on to the south bank of the Mersey estuary towards Widnes and Runcorn, finally joining the great river Mersey at the 'Eastham Locks', probably the biggest, single construction job of the whole canal project.

Eastham had two sets of seaward gates, one to keep the canal in at low tide and an outer pair of storm gates to keep the estuary water out during high tides.

Figure 64 Construction of Eastham Locks

It is said that when Eastham Locks were completed the Chief Engineer said, as he gazed proudly at the Locks **'we saved the best to last'.**

Manchester was finally connected to the Mersey and the 'Irish Sea'.

The first vessel to sail along the thirty six miles of the canal completed the journey on New Year's Day, 1894.

In the summer of 1948, two years after Grandpa had dropped the matchstick into the stream at 'Burnt Edge', Mam, Dad, my sister Sandra and I went on holiday to 'New Brighton'. One sunny morning we walked to the beach. To our right was the 'Mersey' flowing out to the Irish Sea.

Sandra and me were so excited, we had never been to the seaside before. Sandra ran off shouting **"I'm going crabbing in them rock pools"**

Mam spread a towel on the sand and relaxed reading a book, while me and Dad stood looking out to sea, as an ocean liner was approaching the Mersey on it's way to Liverpool. As we stood there fascinated, Dad said **"you know Al, I'll bet that's come all the way from America".**

Just then Sandra shouted from one of the rock pools, **"look at this Dad".** We thought she had caught her first crab, but she was pointing to a little matchstick floating in the pool. I shouted to Mam, who came over to us, and asked **"Mam, d'yer think that's Grandpa's matchstick?"** Mam replied **"I don't know love, but if it is, it's come a long way from 'Brunt Edge'.**

Dad pondered for a while and replied, **"I'll bet it's nearly fifty miles"**. He wasn't far out. Mam smiled, took my hand and said **"don't leave it in that rock pool love, take it to the water's edge and put it into the sea just in case"**. I did just that and the matchstick floated off.

It did finish up in't sea - with a little help. Grandpa was never wrong.